W9-BFY-272

in

Southwestern Ohio

Walks and Rambles

in

Southwestern Ohio

From the Stillwater to the Ohio River

RALPH RAMEY

PHOTOGRAPHS BY THE AUTHOR

Backcountry Publications
Woodstock · Vermont

An invitation to the reader

If you find that conditions have changed along these walks, please let the author and publisher know so that corrections may be made in future printings. Address all correspondence to:

Editor, Walks and Rambles Series
Backcountry Publications
P.O. Box 175
Woodstock, Vermont 05091

Cataloging-in-Publication Data

Ramey, Ralph.
  Walks and rambles in southwestern Ohio : from the Stillwater to the Ohio River / Ralph Ramey ; photographs by the author.
      p.   cm.
  ISBN 0-88150-250-2
  1. Hiking—Ohio—Guidebooks.   2. Ohio—Guidebooks.   I. Title.
GV199.42.03R37   1994
796.5'1'097717—dc20   94-13651
                                                              CIP

Published by Backcountry Publications
A division of The Countryman Press, Inc.
P.O. Box 175
Woodstock, VT 05091

Printed in the United States of America

Book design by Sally Sherman
Maps and calligraphy by Alex Wallach, © 1994
  The Countryman Press, Inc.
Cover and interior photographs by Ralph Ramey
Text composition by Carlson Design Studio

For Professor Richard H. Durrell,
friend and mentor, and teacher to all within the sound of his voice

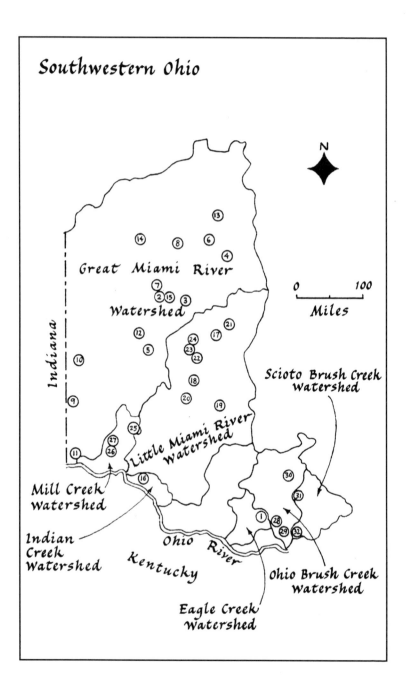

Southwestern Ohio

N

⑬
⑭   ⑧   ⑥
Great Miami River   ④
⑦
②⑮③
Watershed

0   100
Miles

⑫
⑤   ⑰㉑

⑩   ㉔
            ㉓
            ㉒
                    Scioto Brush Creek
⑱   watershed
⑨   ⑳   ⑲

Indiana

㉕
㉗
㉖   Little Miami River
⑪   Watershed
                ⑯
                                    ㉚
Mill Creek
watershed   ㉛

Indian   ① ㉘
Creek   ㉙㉜
Watershed   Kentucky   Ohio River

                                Ohio Brush Creek
                                    watershed
                Eagle Creek
                  Watershed

Contents

Introduction

Footpaths made by humankind have crisscrossed the land of southwestern Ohio for at least 10,000 years. There is good evidence that before the last great continental ice sheet had melted far enough to open the Great Lakes–St. Lawrence River outlet to the sea, hunter-gatherer Native Americans were pursuing woolly mammoths, other mammals, and birds in the valleys and on the broad plains of the area. Later, peoples whose lives were more sedentary lived in the valleys and on the hilltops of southwestern Ohio. They left their distinctive mark on the land in the form of earthworks of all shapes and magnitude and, perhaps, for various purposes. Hundreds of their earthen structures, large and small, simple and highly intricate, dot the southwestern Ohio landscape.

Stories of "Indian-settler" encounters in the Northwest Territory after the United States became a nation are written in the records of that era and in the history books and historical dramas of today. Stories are common about tribes such as the Shawnee, Miami, Erie, Delaware, and Wyandott; tales are recounted about people like Tecumseh, Bluejacket, Chief Logan, Cornstalk, The Prophet, Peter Loramie, Simon Kenton, and Mad Anthony Wayne. Thousands of artifacts have found their ways from the fields of southwestern Ohio to the trays of museums and the walls of collectors. A few of the spots where Indians lived are marked with monuments, but more often the roadside plaques identify places of tragedy for the bronzed people that first occupied Ohio.

Before airplanes and automobiles, train cars and canal boats, and the reintroduction of the horse to North America, everyone traveled on foot or by boat, whether the purpose was to hunt, to move a village a short distance, or to migrate many miles across the continent. With water at both its southern and northern borders, the Ohio country saw much coming and going by Indians, as well as by settlers, in small craft of various type. Still, it was a country primarily of foot travel. Most of the well-traveled trails used by Native Americans and settlers have all but disappeared from the land. A few, like the Simon Kenton trace from Maysville to Springfield, are modern highways. The Ohio Historical Society and a number of local historical groups have preserved special places such as battlefields and earthworks that were once connected by foot trails. Along with the paths and early wagon traces, many of the transportation routes used by nineteenth-century settlers are also in danger of passing from view: canal towpaths, the long-ago abandoned right-of-ways of electric interurban trains, little-used rural roads, and, most recently, the railroad right-of-ways.

Just as the cultural evidence of Native Americans and early settlers has disappeared from the countryside, so, too, has the evidence of the original natural landscape of Ohio nearly vanished. Native grasslands, clean rivers and streams, old-growth forests, fens, bogs, and swamps exist only in "preserves." Most of the walks described here are within such cultural or natural history preserves—areas of special significance protected by the Ohio Department of Natural Resources, the Ohio Historical Society, and local park districts.

For purposes of exploring southwestern Ohio, I have organized this book in accordance with the area's major watersheds, all of which empty into the Ohio River. The 36 walks and rambles, located in 32 areas, have been selected and described to help Ohio families and visitors learn more about the natural and cultural heritage of the area. There is a glossary of geological and botanical terms at the end of the book which defines many of the words used to describe interesting features seen along the trails.

Almost all of these walks are loops of a reasonably short length that can easily be accomplished by youngsters in the company of adults. Some are associated with cultural facilities, such as small, on-site museums; others are graced with interpretive signs along the trails. Good maps and/or pamphlets are sometimes available at the trailheads. Read these in advance since they can add immeasurably to the pleasure of a hike. Too few of these trails are totally accessible to physically challenged visitors, but, thanks to the Americans with

Disabilities Act, more are being adapted for people in wheelchairs and walkers and those with impaired vision each year. Most are public areas, but a few are owned by private, not-for-profit organizations. Nearly all are open year-round without charge, but a few facilities charge a fee and/or restrict hours or entry for part of the year. I nevertheless felt that the latter were of sufficient interest to include here, even though some advance planning may be required for a visit.

Amenities vary, so it is always good to be prepared. Water is easy to carry and a better thirst quencher than soda. Wetlands are wonderful places to study nature, but the walker must be prepared to deal with insects. Light-weight binoculars, camera, pocket compass, hand lens, pencil and spiral-bound pocket notebook for notes, various nature guides (depending upon the site and season), sketchbook and favorite media, small first-aid kit, plastic litter bag to carry out trash, poncho, and trail snacks are all good candidates for a small day pack. With skin cancer on the rise, sunscreen and a hat that will shade your ears and the back of your neck as well as your face are a must for young and old (a ball cap is not enough). Some hikers like a walking stick as a third leg for unbridged stream crossings and rougher terrain travel.

If hiking alone, be sure to tell someone of your plans, including the approximate time you intend to return home. Always lock your car, perhaps even adding a steering-wheel-bar lock. Be sure that nothing of value is visible through the windows of the car that might give someone cause to break a window.

Information about the hiking trails in this book and about other facilities and attractions throughout Ohio can be obtained by calling 1-800-BUCKEYE (282-5393). Agency addresses for the areas described here are as follows:

Aullwood Audubon Center and Farm
1000 Aullwood Road
Dayton, OH 45414-1129
(513) 890-7360

Butler County Park District
2200 Hancock Avenue
Hamilton, OH 45011
(513) 867-5835

Cincinnati Museum of Natural History
1301 Western Avenue
Cincinnati, OH 45203
(513) 287-7000

Dayton-Montgomery County Park District
1375 East Siebenthaler Avenue
Dayton, OH 45414
(513) 278-8231

Greene County Park District
651 Dayton-Xenia Road
Xenia, OH 45385
(513) 376-7445

Hamilton County Park District
10245 Winton Road
Cincinnati, OH 45231
(513) 521-7275

Miami County Park District
2535 East Ross Road
Tipp City, OH 45371
(513) 667-1086

ODNR/Division of Natural Areas and Preserves
1889 Fountain Square Court, F-1
Columbus, OH 43224-1331
(614) 265-6453

ODNR/Division of Parks and Recreation
1952 Belcher Drive, C-3
Columbus, OH 43224-1386
(614) 265-7000

ODNR/Division of Wildlife
1840 Belcher Drive
Columbus, OH 43224-1329
(614) 265-6305

Ohio Historical Society
1982 Velma Avenue
Columbus, OH 43211-2497
(614) 297-2333

Spring Grove Cemetery and Arboretum
4521 Spring Grove Avenue
Cincinnati, OH 45232-1954
(513) 681-6680

Map Legend

Ⓟ parking
● ● ● ● main trail
. . . . . side trail or alternate route
⩘ marsh or swamp
■ building
bridge
paved road
✕ point of interest
◇◇◇ firebreak
🛉 tower (observation, water, etc.)
o‑o‑o‑o bikeway
‑ ‑ ‑ ‑ horse trail

Eagle Creek Watershed

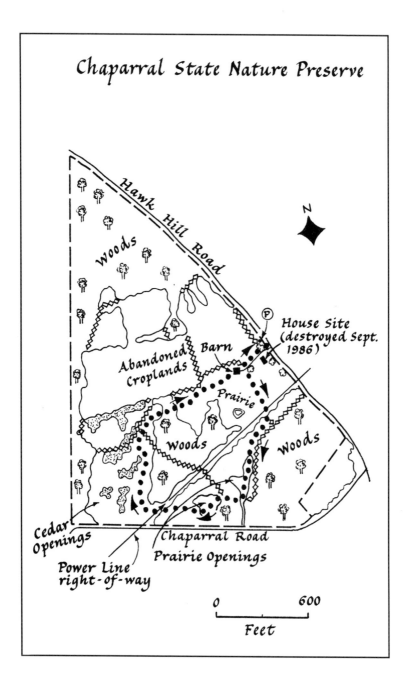

Chaparral State Nature Preserve

Chaparral State Nature Preserve

Distance: 1 mile
Accessibility: Terrain makes access by physically challenged nearly impossible.
Facilities: None

The articles of dedication creating this preserve call for its preservation as a "Blackjack-Post Oak Prairie Opening." That description does not do justice to this very special, 67-acre Adams County preserve. Farmed as recently as 1984, the area is not as highly eroded as other nearby preserves. It has a well-defined trail running through a variety of interesting habitats. A man-made pond near the preserve entrance can be alive with singing male frogs during mating season in the early spring, and nearly a dozen state-listed plant species are found in the area. Management of the preserve is aimed at erasing the vestiges of farming activity and restoring native vegetation. This effort involves periodic late-winter burning of a large expanse of the preserve, an occasional application of a selective herbicide to eliminate undesirable plant species, and hand removal of red cedar (juniper) and some hardwood trees. As in other preserves in the "sweet soil" region of Adams County, the planted forage legumes—yellow and white sweet clover—have become pests that are difficult to eliminate.

In late July and early August, the array of prairie plants here is nothing short of spectacular. The lay of the land allows a sweeping vista of a hillside that, in a year when there has been no drought, will be covered with rattlesnake master, prairie dock, tall coreopsis, and tall blazingstar. (Toward the back of the preserve, the usually purple blazingstar blooms pure white.) Earlier in the summer, the spider milkweed and prairie false-indigo will have dominated the same hillside. Young post oaks and blackjack oaks grow so close to the trail that there is no way they can be missed.

Access

Lying in Tiffin Township in central Adams County, Chaparral Preserve is reached from West Union (the county seat located on OH 125) by traveling north .7 mile on OH 247. You then take Chaparral Road northwest 2.7 miles to where the paved road makes a sharp left turn. Here you take graveled Hawk Hill Road (Township Road 23), which goes straight ahead. There is a small vehicle pulloff on the left side of Hawk Hill Road about .2 mile after the intersection.

Trail

Until 1986, a frame house stood just inside the gate. The only vestiges of that homestead are a metal storage building, an unusable well, and an apple tree. The Hawk Hill Trail originates to the left of the building, just beyond the tree. It goes downhill, then uphill, crossing under a powerline before reaching the edge of the woods on Hawk Hill. This is the sweep of land that is ablaze with prairie forbs during most of the summer, and it is on the right side of the trail as it climbs the hill that the "specimen" post and blackjack oaks grow.

The trail turns right, traveling just inside the woods for a few hundred feet before emerging into the first of two hillside prairie openings. Heading downhill through young woods, it once again passes under the powerline and enters an area of cedar glades and prairie openings. This area is a good spot to see butterflies and several of the special plant species for which the area is known.

Gently climbing uphill, the trail passes through more young woods. It travels through an abandoned field now invaded by prairie grasses as it heads toward the storage building and preserve entrance. The downhill slope to the right of the trail as it approaches the shed is an experimental plot where an herbicide has been applied to control nonnative forage grass. In some years, a large patch of giant ragweed has appeared there. This invasive native annual, one of the principal causes of hayfever, should disappear as the area is repopulated with the perennial prairie grasses.

This walk is one of several to be included in a day's outing in Adams County in the watershed of Ohio Brush Creek. While it is

The Hawk Hill Trail serves as a firebreak during prescribed late-winter burns which encourage the growth of prairie forbs.

most showy in July and August, the preserve holds other treats for the visitor in spring, autumn, and winter. After a short summer shower, you may find yourself sharing the trail with a lumbering eastern box turtle, and (who knows?) you may hear a red-tailed hawk screaming from a treetop on Hawk Hill.

Great Miami River Watershed

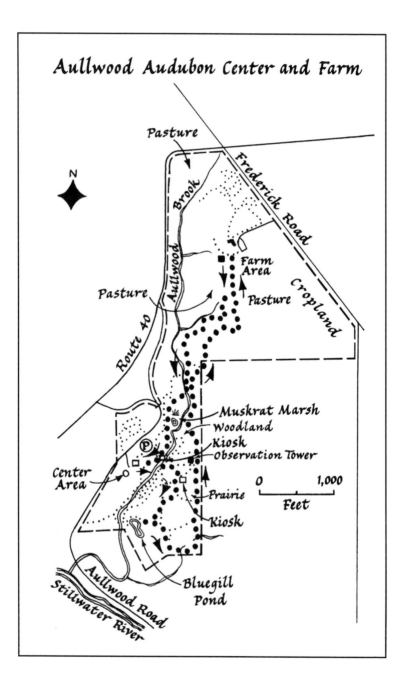

Aullwood Audubon Center and Farm

Pasture

Frederick Road

N

Aullwood Brook

Pasture

Cropland

Farm Area

Route 40

Pasture

Pasture

Muskrat Marsh
Woodland
Kiosk
Observation Tower

P

Center Area

0   1,000
Feet

Prairie

Kiosk

Aullwood Road

Stillwater River

Bluegill Pond

Aullwood Audubon Center and Farm

Distance: 2 miles
Accessibility: Natural surface trails and some steep slopes make
access to this trail by the physically challenged very difficult.
Facilities: Nature center and farm visitor center.
Restroom in both buildings.

Trails that wind past tallgrass prairie, through deep woods, across pasture, and beside ponds, marsh, and stream attract thousands of visitors annually to the National Audubon Society's regional educational center—the 200-acre Aullwood Audubon Center and Farm.

The gift of Mrs. John W. Aull, this community sanctuary and educational resource center works to foster awareness, understanding, and appreciation of the total environment in citizens of all ages. Exhibits at the nature center and in the buildings at the farm interpret natural history and the relationship between humans and the land.

Most of the land remains natural. Its sweet soils, with Ordovician-age limestone close to the surface, grow tall chinquapin and white oaks, hickories, basswood, walnut, ash, and other hardwoods. Huge sycamores mark the course of the stream that crosses the property. A large area has been planted to tallgrass prairie, with burr oak trees planted along one edge.

The farm includes pasture, cropland, vegetable and herb garden, hen house, rabbit hutch, sugarbush, and a magnificent wood bank barn. The latter is a recent replacement for one that was burned to the ground in the late eighties. Horse, cattle, and sheep are among the farm animals that can be seen close-up.

Access

Aullwood is located in Butler and Randolph townships in northern Montgomery County, adjacent to Englewood Reserve of the Park District of Dayton-Montgomery County. To reach it, travel OH 48 north about 1 mile from I-70, then turn east on US 40 and travel a distance of about 1 mile to Aullwood Road (crossing the top of Englewood Dam). Turn right, and the center parking lot is on the left about .2 mile down Aullwood Road.

Except for members of the National Audubon Society and the Friends of Aullwood, there is a small admission charge to Aullwood. The area is open from 9 A.M. to 5 P.M. Monday through Saturday and from 1 to 5 P.M. on Sundays. It is closed on some holidays. The phone number of the administrative office is (513) 890-7360.

Trail

Begin your visit to Aullwood by looking at the displays in the interpretive center. They include live creatures and interactive educational games. From the bird room, you can watch and hear the many feathered (and occasional furred) friends of Aullwood that come to seed and suet feeders.

Slip out the side door of the center and head past the hollow log toward the creek and the Discovery Trail. Stop to read the "cold glacier, warm seas" interpretive sign and to ponder the gathering of glacial erratics to the right of the trail. Sometime you may wish to walk the short Geology Trail that originates here or even hike to the Stillwater River fossil beds. A booklet entitled *Geological Explorations at the Aullwood Audubon Center & Farm* can be purchased in the center.

Cross the creek on the steppingstones or log provided and head through the woods up the gentle slope straight ahead. In April or May you may want to take time to walk the Wildflower Trail that makes a loop to the right. As you emerge from the woods, you will find tallgrass prairie to the right of the trail almost as far as you can see. This vegetation is not indigenous to this site. It is a planted prairie established for educational purposes, using seed gathered from nearby prairie remnants. Managed by occasional prescribed burning in the late winter, it contains dozens of species of the long-

The sycamore's annual rings don't reflect as much variance in growth from normal to drought years as do upland trees, such as oak, because this streamside denizen's roots nearly always reach the water table.

lived perennial grasses and forbs that make up the true prairies of the Midwest. Depending on when you travel the trail, the prairie may look blue-green with splashes of gold and purple, with grass higher than you can reach; it may be dead-looking grass beaten down against the ground by deep snow; or it may contain fresh sprigs of bright green sparkling against blackened soil—the new growth that follows a controlled burn.

   To get a good feel for the prairie, turn right off the Discovery Trail and follow the path to the kiosk, where exhibits tell more about the ecology of Ohio grasslands. Pass around the left end of the shelter, then arc right past a young burr oak tree with prairie on both sides. At a "T" in the trail, go left, then turn right past old fields with bluebird boxes and occasional red cedars to arrive shortly at Bluegill Pond. Listen to the frogs or watch the dragonflies for a time, then return back down the trail to the pond and take the next fork to the right to visit the wet woods.

After you pass plantings of mixed pines and spruce, follow the trail close to the old fencerow into the wet woods. Bush honeysuckle, planted by the droppings of birds, and multiflora rose, moved from fencerows by the same method, are present here and there along the trail. After curving left on the built-up track through the wet woods, turn right and follow the trail along the eastern boundary of the preserve to the prairie tower. This tower is a great place from which to see the total expanse of the Aullwood prairie. A booklet about the prairie is available at the center.

From the tower, take the Center-Farm Trail north through young woods and bush honeysuckle along the boundary heading toward the farm. Several trails exit to the left, but the farm trail continues north near the fence. After ¼ mile of mostly uphill terrain, the trail passes through more mature woods and then turns right to cut across a corner of the park district land. You then veer left to return to Aullwood land and more young woods. Turn right at a well-signed intersection. The trail heads toward the gate as it emerges from the woods. It next follows the edge of a narrow pasture where warm season prairie grasses have been planted. A planting of Scotch pine is visible off to the right. You go up and over the fence on an old-fashioned wooden stile, then across the pasture to the farm area.

Explore the many outbuildings and the visitor center of the barn. Notice that the foundation of the barn is a combination of limestone, such as could be found in nearby streams, and fieldstone—small glacial erratics that had to be cleared from the land before it could be plowed.

Begin your return to the center by retracing the trail into the pasture. Notice the collection of old farm equipment off to the right. Following the edge of the field, you will reach a gate where a sign points right to the center. Turn right, opening and carefully closing the gate. The well-delineated trail swings left, soon crossing a small dam. A bird blind sits off the trail to the left just beyond the pond. From the bird blind, take the Shawnee Trail along the limestone-slab-strewn trail. Following the left bank of the stream, the trail winds down the valley past basswood, cedar, hackberry, and redbud—all species that thrive on the thin soil over limestone. Osage orange betrays the earlier existence of a "hedgeapple" fencerow somewhere close by.

Soon being joined by the Discovery Trail coming in from the left, the Shawnee/Discovery Trail continues downstream. Passing a trail to the right that crosses the stream on stepping-stones, you continue straight ahead, passing station #8 on the Discovery Trail. At a "T", the trail turns right, passing station #7 and then crossing two bridges with a pawpaw patch in between as it moves to the west side of the stream. It soon becomes a four-plank boardwalk traveling through a wetland. It passes stations #6 and #5 and an inoperable pitcher pump before reaching a sidetrail to a pond and Muskrat Marsh. The presence of fen species such as queen-of-the-prairie and Canadian burnet reveal the alkaline nature of the wetland.

After visiting the marsh, return to the main trail. Make a left turn on the boardwalk to continue toward the center. Near station #4, the boardwalk ends. Ignore a side trail that exits to the right and later rejoins from the right, and stay on the Discovery Trail. (A booklet that interprets the numbered stations along the Discovery Trail is available at the center.) Passing large white and chinquapin oaks and many glacial erratics, the trail soon comes to a kiosk where there is a large cross-section of a sycamore. A right turn returns the hiker to the center and parking lot.

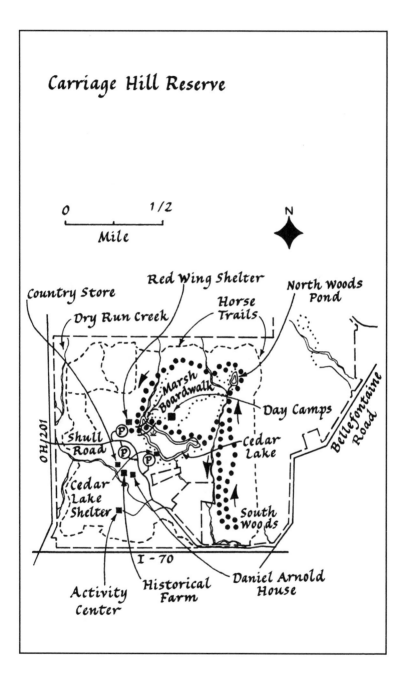

Carriage Hill Reserve

0   1/2

Mile

N

Country Store

Red Wing Shelter

Dry Run Creek

Horse Trails

North Woods Pond

Marsh Boardwalk

Day Camps

OH 201

Shull Road

Cedar Lake

Cedar Lake Shelter

South Woods

Bellefontaine Road

I - 70

Activity Center

Historical Farm

Daniel Arnold House

Carriage Hill Reserve

Distance: 4½ miles
Accessibility: Only elevated boardwalk over wetland at the beginning of trail is accessible to physically challenged.
Facilities: Restrooms, picnic shelters, historical farm, giftshop.

Beginning with an old farm homestead and an idea, the staff of the Park District of Dayton-Montgomery County has turned 1,000 acres of marginal farmland on the northern edge of Montgomery County into a rich cultural and natural history resource center. There, based on the farm life of the Daniel Arnold family, the rural Ohio of the 1880s is being re-created as the Carriage Hill Farm.

Not content to limit development of the reserve to just the historical farm, the district has added a large lake and a small pond where visitors can fish free without a license, two picnic shelters, a boardwalk over a marsh, five miles of hiking trails, and an equal distance of bridle trails.

Carriage Hill is an easy place to spend a few hours or an entire day. At the farm, you can stroll the farmstead and watch as household chores and farming are performed as they were in the 1880s or visit the barn to see the live farm animals. You can enjoy the natural beauty of woodlands, meadows, and water as you hike, fish, picnic, or ride the bridle trails.

Access

Located on the northern border of Montgomery County in Mad River Township, Carriage Hill Reserve is easily reached from I-70. Take OH 201 (Brandt Pike) north less than 1 mile to Shull Road. Turn right to reach the trailhead, then turn left at the second driveway. This drives serves the Red Wing Shelter and is closest to the entrance of the marsh boardwalk.

Trail

A visit to the bulletin board is always a good way to begin a hike, because the local naturalist may have posted the location of interesting seasonal natural events. Some naturalists post lists of what flowers have been seen blooming where and what birds have been seen residing in or moving through the area.

From the bulletin board, you will want to head directly to the entrance to the boardwalk. Step lightly as you move onto it so as not to spook beast or fowl busily fishing or sunning nearby. Frogs, turtles, great blue herons, various species of dabbling ducks, and other furred and feathered creatures are likely to be using the standing and fallen trees along the walk. Stop to read the interpretive sign about life in the marsh. The boardwalk is a little over 100 yards long. It zigzags its way between cottonwood trees as it crosses the marsh at the upper end of Cedar Lake.

Turning right off the end of the boardwalk brings the hiker onto a sometimes muddy trail close to the water, with cattails on the right and old field species, including an occasional red cedar and multiflora rose, to the left. Two trails exit to the left quite close together; in a short distance these trails join to cross the field to the North Woods Pond. Continuing on the shoreline trail, you will soon see in the distance the riprapped earthen dam that creates the impoundment. At the eastern end of the dam, an interpretive sign tells of the need for land stewardship and open grassland. In the late summer, when I walked this trail, the flowers of the many old field plant species were being heavily used by butterflies. A large patch of common milkweed must surely have been used by female monarchs as a place to deposit their tiny green eggs.

At the east end of the lake, where the emergency spillway is visible to the right, make a hard left turn heading northwest. Butterflies were "puddling" in a muddy spot on the trail here when I came by (on a day following an overnight shower). After crossing a short stretch of field, the trail hugs the edge of the woods on the right. Trees, especially the paddle-seeded ash, are moving into the field. Soon, a side trail that you will take to the right enters the woods, crosses the stream on a wooden bridge, then turns right, heading

*A glimpse of a great blue heron from the boardwalk across Cedar Lake
may be in store for the Carriage Hill Reserve hiker.*

almost due south toward the South Woods.

For ½ mile, the trail closely parallels the stream, a branch of
Drylick Run. The regrowth woods through which it runs is full of
many alien plants but also has some nice native wildflowers, such as
the striking patch of late-blooming black-eyed Susans that greeted
me. The sounds of civilization are ever present since I-70 is just
beyond the south boundary, Wright-Patterson Air Force Base lies a
short distance to the southwest, and Cox International Airport, about
the same distance to the west.

Before turning east, the trail drops into a low area where
spotted jewelweed abounds in the summer. After you cross a side
stream on a short bridge, the trail and stream turn to the east. Dying
red cedars are visible among the young hardwoods, evidence that the
area had at one time been cleared and, when abandoned for agriculture, was invaded by red cedar. The latter are now being overtopped
by the deciduous trees that follow in new growth forest. Occasional

osage orange trees remain as testimony to the earlier use of this Ozarkian species as living fences.

Now heading uphill in a northwesterly direction, the trail soon reaches a large ash tree as it passes close to the corner of an open field to the east. Moving north now a hundred feet or less inside the young woods, the trail passes through a stand of red cedars where there is a large patch of purple coneflower.

After crossing a short bridge, the trail ascends a ridge, which it follows for a short time before moving to the left, closer to the stream. In fact, the trail may become a stream during storms. At a "T" in the trail, turn right to circumnavigate North Woods Pond. You may want to take the next trail left as far as the earthen dam to look for wood ducks or to take a picture, but return to the main trail to move counterclockwise up the east side through the woods. Ignore the side trails that fishermen take to the places wherein they are certain the lunkers lie in wait.

At the north end of the pond, a short wooden bridge spans the stream. The trail you take to the right passes an open area, then winds through young woods before being joined by a trail from the left. It crosses another wooden bridge and emerges into open meadow.

Following a mowed path, the trail heads west, then south, before forking. Take the right fork downhill, where a half dozen tall cottonwood trees tower over the younger trees of the stream-side forest. Glacial erratics are visible beside the trail, probably brought there from nearby cultivated fields on a stone boat by an early farmer. Beyond the stream, the trail turns south, passing under some fine white oak trees. Soon it rises onto a low ridge to the right, then emerges from the woods to parallel the cottonwoods that line the upper end of Cedar Lake. You are now heading toward the picnic shelter and parking lot.

Though I finished hiking this trail in a cracking, booming thunderstorm, I enjoyed it very much. I was accompanied in the woods by calling treefrogs and many edge-dwelling species of birds and, until the storm came, across the open fields by butterflies and dragonflies. The mosquitos were minimal, and the variety of summer wildflowers in bloom, a pleasant surprise.

Cedar Bog
Nature Preserve

Distance: 1½ miles
Accessibility: About eighty yards of grass and wood
chip trail at the beginning. The remainder is all
accessible boardwalk but is elevated and without edgeboards.
Facilities: Information shelter and
nonaccessible portable toilets.

Many people refer to Cedar Bog as Ohio's premier nature preserve. With its combination of fen and white cedar stand, it is, in the true sense of the word, unique. Simply in sheer numbers of state-listed plant and animal species that have been found there, with additional ones still being reported, it stands head and shoulders above other preserves. Published studies of the area date back to at least 1920, and it has been officially protected since 1942 when the state purchased 100 acres for management by the Ohio (Archaeological and) Historical Society.

The wetlands in this preserve are all that remains of a wet prairie-fen complex that at one time covered at least 600 acres along Cedar Run in the broad valley of the Mad River north of Springfield. Early in the twentieth century, the Mad River was channelized for most of its length and ditches dug and tiles installed in an attempt to make the entire valley tillable. A major tributary of the Great Miami River, the Mad runs clear and cold because of the many springs that make up its source. Attempts to drain the headwaters of spring-fed Cedar Run never met with success.

Once accessed with great difficulty, the quicksandlike wetland of this preserve can now be easily viewed from a 1½ mile-long boardwalk. Expanded from the original purchase to 427 acres with the help of The Nature Conservancy and the Division of Natural Areas and Preserves of the Ohio Department of Natural Resources, the preserve includes swamp forest, marl meadow, sedge meadow, arbor vitae forest, and original and reestablished prairie. Studies of the hydrogeology, microclimate, ecology, and flora and fauna of the preserve continue.

The field notes from my first visit to this area on October 16, 1948, refer to it as Dallas Arbor Vitae Swamp. When first acquired by the historical society, it was called Cedar Swamp. A decade or so later, the name was changed to Cedar Bog. Though retaining that name, the nonforested part of the preserve that is wetland is now generally referred to as a fen because of the origin and alkalinity of its water.

A walk through Cedar Bog with an interpretive naturalist is an exciting adventure into Ohio's past. It is a remnant of the vegetation of a postglacial time when the climate of Ohio was considerably cooler. In addition, it is a refugium for other plant and animal species that invaded Ohio during a dry, warm period that occurred as recently as three or four thousand years ago. All species blend together in a special mixture of habitats not found in the same combination anywhere else.

Your guide will explain to you how scientists believe that this area remained unchanged while eastern hardwood forest covered most of the state. You will learn about the source of the alkaline water upon which the fen "floats" and perhaps have an opportunity to jump up and down on the soil surface to set the ground shaking. The special relationships between plants and animals and the fen and forest environment will come alive when you observe them firsthand. Five of the six species of swallowtail butterfly found in Ohio frequently can be seen in the preserve, for the food plants of all five grow there. The spotted turtle with its yellow-spotted black shell survives in the bog because it can avoid freezing during the winter by hibernating and can avoid overheating in the summer by aestivating in the even-temperatured muck under the surface of the bog.

Like so many preserves, threats from the pressures of human endeavors are no stranger to Cedar Bog. In the seventies, construction of a four-lane highway to be built alongside the preserve was halted. Nevertheless, nearby development, reconsideration of high-

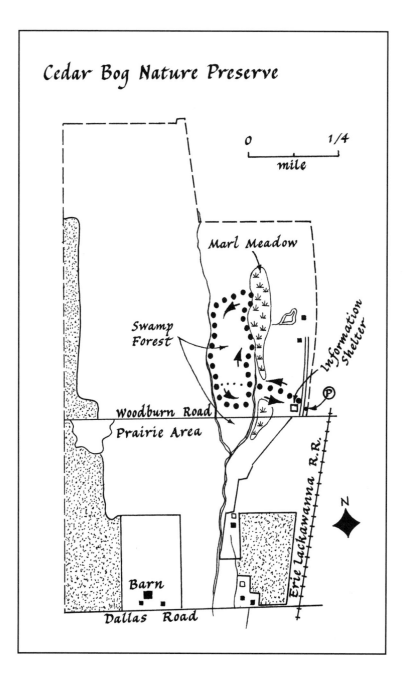

Shortly after entering the woods at Cedar Bog, the trail crosses the east branch of Cedar Run, a place where, on a rare occasion, a spotted turtle might be seen basking on a log.

way construction, overutilization of the underlying aquifer, air pollution, and global warming all threaten to accelerate the demise of this special place. Alien plants such as bush honeysuckle and garlic mustard, which grow well on the fertile soil of the preserve, threaten to displace the native flora. Raccoons, with no predators and only disease to keep their numbers under control, pose a threat to the rare spotted turtles.

The Ohio Historical Society, with advice from many scientists in the Department of Natural Resources and from others around the country, apply modern management techniques to try to prevent the loss of special species and habitat. Cedar seedlings that threaten to shade out populations of rare plants have been removed by hand, and programs have been instituted to control plant and animal pests.

Access

Located in Urbana Township near the southern boundary of Champaign County, Cedar Bog Nature Preserve is easily reached by traveling 1 mile west on Woodburn Road from US 68, approximately 4.5 miles south of the center of Urbana.

Except for members of the Ohio Historical Society or the Cedar Bog Association, there is a small admission charge. The area is open to visitation only during public tours, which are conducted by a naturalist at 1 and 3 P.M. Saturdays and Sundays from April through September. Group tours between 9 A.M. and 5 P.M. Wednesdays though Sundays from April through September can be arranged by calling (513) 484-3744. For group tours during other months, call the same number or (in Ohio) 1-800-686-1541. Access to trails without a guide is prohibited.

The bog is a permanent wetland where mosquitos as well as deer flies are often present in large numbers during the warm months of the year. Do not enter the bog unprepared. The uncommon massasauga rattlesnake also makes its home in the preserve, but it is extremely unlikely that this small, nonaggressive snake will be seen let alone encountered by a visitor.

Trail

The trail into Cedar Bog begins on the left side of the driveway, just beyond the information kiosk. The approach to the boardwalk is mowed grass and wood chip trail several hundred feet long. In midsummer, a number of plant species such as joe-pye weed, bergamot, black-eyed Susan, New England aster, and thistles that are especially attractive to butterflies bloom in the old fields alongside the entry trail.

Upon reaching the boardwalk, the hiker will immediately be surrounded by the white cedar (arbor vitae) for which the bog is named. From early spring to late summer there are dozens of species of wildflowers that line the trail. To try to list them all, let alone place them in the location and sequence in which they will be seen, would be a quite impossible task. Blooming skunk cabbage opens the show in late February before the last frost of spring and fringed gentian closes it in late September or October after the first frost of fall. In between come the beds of marsh marigolds and golden ragworts of April, the trilliums and jack-in-the-pulpits of May, the showy lady's-slipper of June, the marl meadow plants of July, and the prairie plants of August. At no time between the last frost of spring and the first frost of autumn will there not be a flower in bloom. Note that, because of the cooler microclimate of the bog, the "growing season" is considerably shorter than that recorded at the local weather station and frost has been recorded in nearly every month.

Several hundred feet into the bog and after crossing the East Branch of Cedar Run, the boardwalk reaches an intersection where, beneath the limbs of a large, multitrunked tuliptree, it goes right, left, and straight ahead. Your guide will most likely lead you to the right to travel through the swamp forest. Once considered an elm-ash-maple association, the elm is gone except for an occasional young tree that has yet to succumb to Dutch elm disease. Tuliptree is now a codominant species with ash and the soft maples in this environment.

The trail soon emerges from the forest to pass though arbor vitae hummock, marl meadow, and sedge meadow. Wide platforms along the trail provide places to gather around your guide to learn more about the unique habitats. After winding north parallel to the East Branch of Cedar Run, the boardwalk turns west and then heads south along the West Branch. There it runs atop a spoil bank where earth was dumped when the creek was dredged in an unsuccessful attempt to drain the bog for "muck farming" in the early part of the century. It is along this reach that, in the spring, I have some years seen a spotted turtle basking on a log.

Shortly before reaching the chain-link fence along Woodburn Road, the trail turns east, then north through the swamp forest to return to the main intersection. There is a shorter cut-off trail that runs from east to west across the middle of the preserve, but most visitors cover the entire loop with their guide.

A walk through Cedar Bog is an experience you will not soon forget. Since first visiting the area in 1948, I have returned to explore the bog hundreds of times, finding some small reward during each visit. This is a treasure that everyone interested in the natural world should get to know.

Cox Arboretum

Distance: 1¼ miles
Accessibility: No access to the natural area trails by
physically challenged, although the horticultural
plantings, buildings, and all other facilities
of the arboretum are accessible.
Facilities: Arboretum, horticultural plantings, visitor
center, gift shop, restrooms, and drinking water.

Behind the groves of flowering trees and shrubs and the neatly manicured gardens of Dayton's Cox Arboretum lies an area where nature rules. Gravel trails wind their way among fields and forests of the hillside that slopes west to busy I-75 and the densely populated Great Miami River valley.

Begun by a small group of people interested in creating an arboretum for the citizens of Dayton, Cox Arboretum is now one of the eight reserves of the tax-supported Park District of Dayton-Montgomery County. With help from a private foundation, membership support, and hundreds of volunteers, Cox Arboretum brings year-round pleasure to those who love plants. Here plants are cultivated for education and for the pure pleasure that their beauty brings to all who see them.

The cultivated gardens and the plantings of crabapples, conifers, and other woody plants occupy only about one-third of the 159 acres of the reserve. The rest is designated as natural area, with 1½ miles of foot trails open to the public.

Access

Cox Arboretum is located at 6733 Springboro Pike (OH 741) in Miami Township, Montgomery County. Its entrance is not quite 1 mile north of OH 725 on the west side of the road. The grounds are open from 8 A.M. until dusk every day of the year except Christmas and New Year's Day. Pets are not allowed.

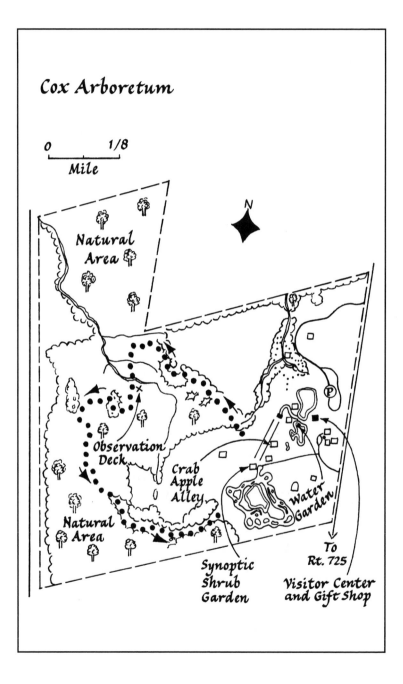

Cox Arboretum

0   1/8
Mile

N

Natural Area

Natural Area

Observation Deck

Crab Apple Alley

Synoptic Shrub Garden

Water Garden

P

To Rt. 725

Visitor Center and Gift Shop

Trail

A good place to begin walking the trails of Cox Arboretum is at the Visitor Center. Come out the front door, make a right turn around the building, cross the bridge between the two ponds of the Water Garden, and turn right, following the rock wall as it curves south to enter Crab Apple Alley. After passing about twenty pairs of trees, exit right and walk to the edge of the mowed grass where there is a sign that says, quite simply, "trail."

An eight-foot-wide gravel trail leads into the woods where, to the right of the trail, you can study a large map of the area or pick up a trail map to carry with you. The trail winds downhill through woodland made up of many species. The presence of red cedars, blue ash, redbud, and hackberry indicates the calcareous nature of the bedrock that lies just below the surface of this eroded hillside. As in so many of the woodlands of western Ohio, much of the shrub layer is the alien bush honeysuckle.

At the first trail juncture, a bench sits under a large juniper tree. Take the trail to the right and continue around the hillside. Some of the cedars show evidence of a grass fire. Side-oats grama and little bluestem, grasses of dry prairies, show up here and there in the cedar thickets.

Beyond the cedar openings, the trail goes downhill through a nice woodland and nearly levels out before crossing a small gully on a bridge. It then continues through more woods. On the hillside beside the trail lies a glacial erratic reminding us that, even though bedrock is close to the surface here, the area was glaciated. How else would a granite boulder make it to this remote hillside in Montgomery County, Ohio? Strategically placed benches tempt the hiker to linger, but if quiet is what is desired, this is hardly the spot; the highway noise from the interstate below is ever audible.

Soon the trail reaches a larger gully where there is an observation deck. Steps lead down to the creek, where you cross on slabstones before going up more steps to another deck. The view upstream from the deck must be very enjoyable when water is tumbling over the layers of limestone in the creekbed.

Just beyond, the trail makes a juncture with a trail to the left that goes uphill to return to the trailhead. Turning right takes the

Dry much of the year, this creek carries a torrent of water from the grounds of Cox Arboretum upslope during a summer downpour.

hiker around the hillside through a shrubby area, past cedar thicket, then through a woodland with some trees of up to two feet in diameter. Side trails to the right are best ignored because they go closer to the noisy highway and head downhill, making the climb to the trail's end more difficult.

As the trail arcs left and uphill in its return to the arboretum area, it passes another cedar thicket; this one is graced with a well-written interpretive sign telling of the role of cedars in the natural environment (as opposed to use in chests, closets, and souvenirs). Still climbing gently, the trail goes through a bush honeysuckle alley and past more old field before emerging onto the mowed lawn near the Synoptic Shrub collection. Go around the left side of this shrub collection and head for Crab Apple Alley to return to the Visitor Center, now in view beyond the Water Garden lake.

Each trail in this area holds a certain beauty and tells a tale of its own. Trying to determine the past history of the use of the land by reading the landscape of the present is always fun and a challenge. The trail at Cox Arboretum is a good place to sharpen that skill.

Davey Woods
State Nature Preserve

Distance: 1½ miles
Accessibility: The steep terrain and natural trail
surface precludes access by the physically challenged.
Facilities: Bulletin board only. Kiser Lake State Park
is located nearby, just north of St. Paris on OH 235.
It has restrooms, picnic tables, and a campground.

Abowhunter's camp once sat close to the parking lot for this preserve. There were targets scattered throughout the woods and at least one deer observation platform mounted in the trees. These are all gone, and the area is presently closed to hunting of any sort, protected as a state nature preserve for enjoyment by all creatures, large and small.

Dedicated as an interpretive preserve in 1990, Davey Woods was acquired through a cooperative project with the Ohio Chapter of The Nature Conservancy. It was purchased at a bargain price with half of the funding coming from a contribution by the Davey Tree Expert Company of Kent, Ohio, and the other part from the Ohio State Income Tax Check-off Fund. Triangular in shape, this 104-acre preserve is on a hillside facing the valley of Nettle Creek, a Mad River (hence, Great Miami River) tributary.

The area has been studied extensively by Dr. Ralph Boerner and his students from Ohio State University. Though not a virgin forest, it is considered to be an excellent example of a mixed mesophytic community of the eastern hardwood forest biome. No endangered or threatened plant species have been recorded in the preserve. There are some occurrences of pest plant species such as bush honeysuckle, garlic mustard, and barberry, but the problem is not extensive. Deer frequent the woods, but many are harvested on neighboring lands so that no flora-threatening build-up of the deer herd has yet occurred.

Several species of owls have been heard calling in the woods, and hawks have been known to nest in the tall trees. Two trails have been developed, the Short Loop Trail of slightly less than a half mile and the longer Conrad Trail of just over a mile, named for a previous landowner. They interconnect and together provide a nice walk that is completely within the woods.

Access

Davey Woods is located in Concord and Mad River townships in central Champaign County. From Urbana, travel 7 miles west on US 36 to Neal Road. Go north 1 mile to Smith Road, then west .5 mile to Lonesome Road. The parking lot is on the left side of the road, approximately .2 mile northwest of the Smith Road intersection. The preserve is open during daylight hours. If the gate is locked, park outside the gate but do not block it.

Trails

After checking the bulletin board, start hiking by turning left off the end of the parking lot and crossing the wooden bridge over a small creek. Turn left at the end of the bridge and follow the trail around the hillside above Lonesome Road, climbing most of the way. The trail soon turns west and tops a low ridge before dropping into the valley of the stream it had crossed earlier. A trail to the right, heading downstream on the side of the hill, completes the Short Loop Trail by recrossing the bridge to the parking lot.

By turning left, upstream and away from the bridge, the hiker starts the Conrad Trail, headed around the perimeter of the preserve. Less than ¼ mile up the valley, the trail crosses the now much narrower stream and ascends to the higher ground along the western edge of the preserve. Occasionally dipping to cross small streambeds, the trail continues north about ⅓ mile, passing some large trees and some areas where young trees are reclaiming once-cleared land. One spot near the west boundary is noticeably devoid of shrubs, possibly serving as a deer yard during the winter.

The trail turns gradually to the east, then southeast as it begins its descent to the trailhead. It passes a spot where at one time a home

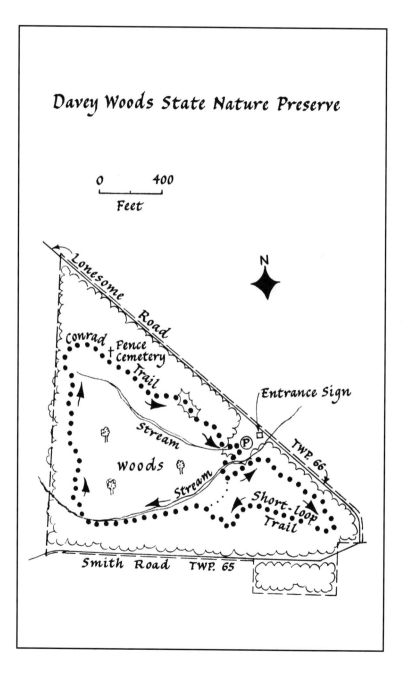

Davey Woods State Nature Preserve

The trails at Davey Woods begin on a footbridge of a normally peaceful, but during storms, a powerful stream.

must have stood, as evidenced by the apple trees that remain. Likely deer enjoy the apples in the autumn. A single red cedar looks as if it might have been planted near a homestead rather than being a remnant of a cedar thicket. There is also a pioneer burial ground located not far off the trail. As the trail continues downhill parallel to Lonesome Road, some large, open-grown sugar maples and tuliptrees can be seen down the slope below. As it approaches the parking lot, the trail follows a streambed. You cross a three-foot bridge over the stream, which has turned to head toward Lonesome Road and Nettle Creek in the distance.

This trail provides for a not-too-challenging walk in a setting where there is not likely to be a crowd. On the late summer evening when I hiked it, there were very few mosquitos, and the only sounds came from a cacophonic chorus of tree crickets, katydids, and the like, and the plaintiff call of wood peewees close by.

Englewood Reserve

Distance: ¾ mile
Accessibility: Rocky terrain and uneven natural trail surface
make access by physically challenged impossible.
Facilities: Restrooms, picnic tables and shelters, drinking
water, bikeway, riding center and bridle trails,
fishing, sledding hill, river access.

After the waters of the 1913 flood receded from downtown Dayton, the city fathers began looking for a way to prevent a recurrence. Their answer came in the creation of the Miami Conservancy District, the hiring of Arthur Morgan as chief engineer, and the eventual construction of five unique flood control structures on the Great Miami River and four of its principal tributaries. These earthen dams were built with permanent concrete openings where the main channel of the river flows through. When a storm event occurs, water backs up behind the dam while a measured amount of water insufficient to cause flooding downstream continues to flow through the gate. When the storm ceases, the water continues draining out, eventually returning to its normal flow. Between periods of high water, the land behind the dam is used for recreation and agriculture.

Englewood Dam, built in 1922, is the Miami Conservancy District's flood control structure on the Stillwater River. In 1967, the Park District of Dayton-Montgomery County leased 532 acres from the conservancy and has since added 948 acres more to their Englewood Reserve. This land provides a major outdoor recreation facility for the people of Montgomery and surrounding counties.

The task of building Englewood Dam was formidable. One obstacle was in rerouting US 40, the National Road. This road, begun in 1825 as a dirt road, was the primary link between the East

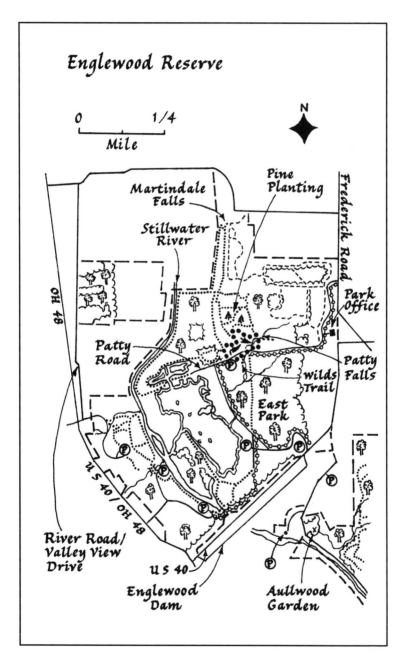

Englewood Reserve

and the West and was often referred to as "Mainstreet U.S.A." The next task was to select a site suitable for the innovative design of the dam and to procure the land. One chosen tract was the 100-acre Patty farm that had been in the same family since 1829. Charles Patty, his wife Phoebe Pearson Patty, and his brother, James, had left Union, South Carolina in 1812 and headed for Ohio. At that time, Ohio had been a state for fewer than ten years and was still mostly wilderness. Three generations of Pattys left their mark on the land, the evidence of which you will glimpse as you walk the trail described here.

The Patty Falls Trail is but one of several good hiking trails in Englewood Reserve. A printed trail guide for this particular hike is available, usually in a box at the trailhead or obtainable from the park district office or a ranger on duty.

Access

The reserve is along the northern edge of Montgomery County, mostly in Butler Township although the area west of the Stillwater River is in Randolph Township.

The entrance to the one-way Englewood Reserve main road is north off US 40 at the east end of Englewood Dam, just east of the city of Englewood. It is directly opposite Aullwood Road, which leads to the Aullwood Audubon Center.

From US 40, drive north on the park road (forking toward the right to avoid going to the lake), then head east (right) on Patty Road to the first parking lot on the right. A restroom, bulletin board, drinking water, and picnic shelter are all within sight. The trailhead lies across Patty Road from the parking area, where a sign announces "hiking trail."

Trail

At the trail entrance is a dispenser for trail guides. You will enjoy and learn from the interpretation this guide provides. The numbered posts face the hiker who is traveling counterclockwise on this loop trail.

The trail starts on a six-foot-wide gravel path through young forest, with an occasional old tree mixed in. Almost level at first, the trail passes the first post on the self-guided trail and soon begins to rise gently. A side trail to the left goes to a meadow. One hundred feet ahead, the trail splits with the trail straight ahead leading to Martindale Falls, not quite one mile to the north, and to the River Trail. Take the trail to the right, which leads to the Pine area and Patty Falls. This wide path goes gently uphill, curving to the left past the second self-guided trail post. This is a young forest, probably less than the age of the dam. Typical of protected areas, there is evidence of the presence of white-tailed deer, with game trails throughout but with minimal destruction to the herbaceous and shrub layers.

Curving to the left, the trail gets steeper before reaching another intersection, with the left trail headed toward the pine management area. Take the Patty Falls Trail to the right. There is a small map shelter at this junction. Limestone bedrock is exposed here, which should come as no surprise since the trees that do well on limestone have been much in evidence from the start—hackberry, basswood, chinquapin oak, and redbud to name but a few.

Twenty-five feet after forking to the right, the Patty Falls Trail makes another right turn. The third self-guided trail post is on the left shortly after this turn. Glacial erratics on both sides of the trail remind the hiker that this land was covered by the most recent glacier. The numbers of erratics here indicate they were cleared from the fields and pushed into the ravines to help make the land arable. The trail now moves through oak-maple forest. There are some magnificent old sugar maples in this area that somehow missed the woodsman's axe.

As the trail follows the edge of the valley, self-guided station #4 draws attention to two tall, forest-grown, wild black cherry trees. This land was probably never tilled but rather used by the Patty family for pasture. There is also a nice tall basswood close by here.

If the rainfall has been good, Patty Falls is audible from this point. The trail begins dropping, now passing a number of oaks measuring about three feet in diameter at breast height. When the trail veers right, you begin walking directly on bedrock. A trail comes in from the left to join the Patty Falls Trail, now crossing the top of the falls. The presence of myrtle on the forest floor reminds

Englewood Reserve's Patty Falls trail passes beneath the old National Road through a stone culvert built more than a century ago.

you that this was not always wilderness; a homestead or church must once have stood nearby. The Patty family doubtless used this stream as their source of water. Be careful crossing the top of the falls, even when they are virtually dry.

Pawpaws grow next to the trail, as do wild hydrangeas. Ignore the trail coming in from the left (not on the trail map) just beyond the falls crossing. Take the limestone steps down to the viewing platform. Notice the calcite build-up on the falls to the right of the viewing platform, just like stalactites in a cave—the result of dissolved limestone in the water flowing over the falls.

Climb back up the steps from the falls and turn right to follow the trail past self-guided trail station #5 and downhill toward the old National Road (now called Patty Road). At the bottom of the 35 steps, turn right and follow the trail through the stone arch bridge under the old highway. Trail station #6 is located here. Note the bridge construction, with the stone blocks being placed on oak planks to prevent undercutting of the limestone. The stone blocks for the arch were probably quarried very close by. In the event of high water under the bridge, detour up and over.

Fifty feet beyond the stone arch bridge, beneath a large hack-berry tree, stands another small map shelter. To the left is the Wilds Trail. Take the trail to the right that heads to the picnic area and parking lot, passing a beautiful three-foot-plus diameter chinquapin oak. At an open area where grape vine seems to be taking over, self-guided trail sign #7 identifies a good spot to talk about forest succession.

After passing an area of old field summer wildflowers and crossing a new culvert, the trail passes another map shelter. A foot-ball field away is the parking lot and trailhead. The stone structure of the picnic area was probably built by the Civilian Conservation Corps in the late 1930s.

Be sure to turn uphill as you leave the parking lot, as Patty Road is still one-way at this point. You will pass over the old stone arch bridge and some speed bumps before arriving at the entrance to the park office, where the road becomes two-way. Watch for riders on horses crossing the road in this area.

Garbry's
Big Woods

Distance: .7 mile
Accessibility: Accessible, but 42-inch-wide boardwalk
with no edgeboards and few passing areas.
Facilities: Accessible picnic tables, well water,
and grills. No restrooms.

For reasons that have gone with them to their graves, the men of Miami County's Garbry family chose not to clear the "big woods" on their farm. In an era of fireplaces and woodburning stoves, the woods was surely a good source of fuel for the Garbry home located nearby; likely sweet sap from its giant maples sated the family sweet tooth on many a cold winter's morn. From cradle to coffin, household necessities were probably fashioned from an occasional cherry, walnut, or oak tree. But they did not completely clear the land, and in 1981 the late J. Scott Garbry made certain it would never be cleared by donating 100 acres of the 150-acre "big woods" the family had saved to the Miami County Park District as part of a new 272-acre park. A sanctuary for young Garbry growing up on a farm, the woods will now remain so in perpetuity for all to know and enjoy as he did.

Lying on poorly drained land just west of Lost Creek in the watershed of the Great Miami River, Garbry's Big Woods is a wet area with standing water during much of the spring and places where the water remains year-round. In February the shrill call of the eastern wood frog advertises from the pond for a mate, and in December the early nesting great-horned owl breaks the silence over a blanket of snow as he seeks the same. In a woods filled with flowers from early spring to late fall, creatures with fur, feather, and scale live out their lives. Large enough to provide adequate-sized territory away from the dangerous wood's edge where predators abound, Big

Woods is the summer home to many Neotropical bird species such as warblers, vireos, flycatchers, and thrushes. When the resident pileated woodpeckers or barred owls break the silence with their loud calls, all human visitors stop to take note. During the middle of the summer, the plaintiff song of the wood peewee or the melodious call of the wood thrush will give special pleasure to the early evening walker.

Built in 1986 by park district employees, a ¾-mile-long board-walk takes visitors into the deep woods where they can experience the drama of nature. With wooden benches on "conversation nodes" spaced at intervals along the trail, Big Woods is a marvelous place to go to spend an hour or a day at any time of the year. Trees and flowers along the trail are labeled, making it a good place to learn the local flora. During spring wildflower season and at the peak of bird migration, park district naturalists conduct scheduled interpretive walks.

As a wet woods, throughout the warm months Big Woods produces an almost continuous hatch of mosquitos that feed the birds and, themselves, seek for something on which to feed. Proper protective clothing and/or repellent should be a part of every hiker's kit bag.

Access

Garbry's Big Woods is located in Spring Creek Township in central Miami County. To reach it, travel east from I-75 on US 36 to Union-Shelby Road. Go south 1 mile then turn east on Statler Road and travel .5 mile to the sanctuary entrance on the south side of the road.

Trail

The boardwalk starts from the center of the south side of the parking lot. Off to the left, a permanent pond soon comes into view. During the spring, pause for a few moments to allow the frogs to resume their calling. Perhaps a family of wood ducks will be swimming there. Even with a relatively large deer herd in the area, the herbaceous flora is in good shape. Both drooping and large-flowered trillium bloom along the trail in the spring. In the late summer, white

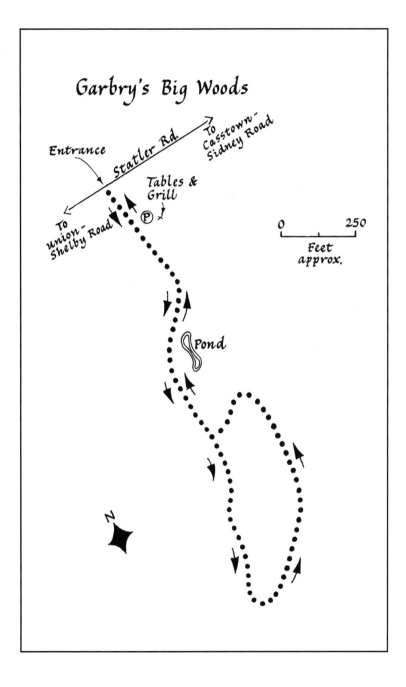

Where the trail in the sanctuary at Garbry's Big Woods splits to become a loop, a bronze bas-relief of the donor of the lovely woods greets the visitor.

snakeroot is among those few plant species that will flower in the shade of this deep wood. This plant, of course, is the one that brought so much grief to settlers until they learned that the condition known as milk fever was caused by drinking milk from cows that had fed on snakeroot.

Spicebush is common in the shrub layer, and pawpaw is among the understory trees; consequently, the spicebush swallowtail and the zebra swallowtail whose larvae feed from these species should be among the butterflies found nectaring in nearby open fields. A stand of bladdernut trees is a pleasant surprise. The trees of the forest canopy, composed of many species, are tall forest-grown trees, many with their first branches far from the ground.

Soon after entering the woods, the trail splits to become a loop. On a stone cairn there is a bronze bas-relief of Scott Garbry standing against a tree. An inscription reads, "God is love for earth as our life belongs as much to those who come after us as to us."

Many of the areas along the boardwalk that hold water in the spring are dry during the summer, with good stands of nettles. They are not friendly to those who might wander off the trail, but they are the larval food plant for many butterflies such as the red admiral, comma, and Milbert's tortoiseshell.

The weeping, sun-warmed wax below a hole on a tall beech betrays the presence of bees. Rows of holes on another tree are the work of sapsuckers. As I walked the trail one midsummer day, a five-lined skink scampered along the planks a few yards ahead of me. These are but a few of the treasures this trail holds for those who walk it today and those yet unborn who will be able to follow in our footsteps thanks to the vision of J. Scott Garbry. Enjoy.

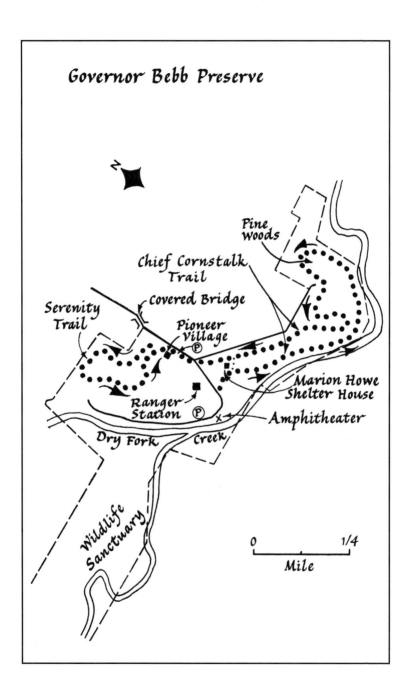

Governor Bebb Preserve

Pine woods

Chief Cornstalk Trail

Covered Bridge

Serenity Trail

Pioneer Village

Ⓟ

Ranger Station

Ⓟ

Marion Howe Shelter House

Amphitheater

Dry Fork   Creek

Wildlife Sanctuary

0   1/4
Mile

Governor Bebb Preserve

Distance: 1½ miles
Accessibility: Trail is inaccessible to physically challenged, but the Pioneer Village area is accessible.
Facilities: Campground, restrooms, drinking water, picnic shelter, pioneer village, youth hostel.

William Bebb, a native son of Butler County, was the nineteenth governor of the state of Ohio. A member of the Whig party, he served from 1846 to 1848. It was a stormy period in Columbus. Under his governorship, construction of the capitol building, begun in 1839, was restarted after several years of delay due to a financial crunch caused in part by a canal bond scandal. Work continued on the capitol building after Bebb left office, but construction was slow and it was not completed until 1861.

In 1959, Governor Bebb Preserve was established to serve as a site for the restored log house of his birth. The park is located on the floodplain of and hillside above Dry Run Fork at its confluence with Sater Run, both streams originating in Indiana. Dry Run Fork is a tributary of the Whitewater River, which joins the Great Miami River about six miles above the latter's confluence with the Ohio River.

Later on, when a wooden covered bridge of an unusual design that spanned Indian Creek west of Oxford needed to be replaced, it was moved to a site on the edge of Governor Bebb Park where it would carry no traffic.

A nonprofit Governor Bebb Preserve Pioneer Group assists the Butler County Park District with improvements, maintenance, and programming at the park. It sponsors several seasonal events such as the annual Green Up Day, Pioneer Days, a Halloween Haunted

Forest, and a Pioneer Christmas. During the summer months, volunteers are present on Sunday afternoons to lead visitors through the Pioneer Village.

Access

Governor Bebb Preserve is located off OH 126 (Cincinnati-Brookville Road) in Morgan Township of Butler County, about 3 miles west of the village of Okean and 1 mile east of Scipio, Indiana, at the Ohio-Indiana line. The .6-mile entry drive runs south off of the highway. The park is open without charge during daylight hours throughout the year.

Trails

Enter the park, pass the covered bridge and Pioneer Village, and travel down the hill to the parking lot on the right side of the drive near the ranger station. Begin your exploration of the park by first walking the Chief Cornstalk Trail. It begins on the opposite side of the drive from the ranger station and heads downstream. The floodplain through which it passes is at first broad, then, as Dry Fork Creek swings back toward the hillside, becomes quite narrow. The trees are typical bottomland species such as cottonwood and box elder. Chinquapin oak, blue ash, and hackberry reveal the presence of calcareous bedrock close to the surface. Sand underfoot on the trail indicates that Dry Fork Creek often covers this bottomland.

Numbers on channel posts seem to indicate the existence of a self-guided trail brochure, but none were available at the trailhead. The woods comprises mostly young trees. After paralleling the stream for less than ½ mile, the trail turns left to climb the hillside at a comfortable angle. Limestone outcrops occur along the trail on the hillside. A large, open-grown white oak tree, perhaps a couple hundred years old, at the top of the rise is helping to provide seeds for regenerating the hillside forest.

At the corner of a pine plantation, an arrow invites the hiker to turn right and take a loop trail around the pines and back to the Cornstalk Trail. Like so many pines, these were planted at eight-foot intervals, a good spacing for Christmas trees but not for a plantation

Vehicle traffic no longer rumbles across the wooden roadbed
of the covered bridge at Governor Bebb Preserve.

that will be allowed to grow beyond six- or eight-feet tall. When planted, they were probably all the same age and size, but now some have trunks twice the diameter of others, evidence of the dominance of some canopies over others. Removing the smaller diameter trees would allow the others to develop more fully. After passing a bench, the trail turns left to go up the right side of a small ravine. On the left, hardwoods appear to be invading the edge of the pine plantation. There are more pines ahead on the right, along with an occasional juniper and with trees and shrubs that look like they came from a Soil and Water Conservation District "wildlife packet." Continue following the trail counterclockwise around the pine grove.

Glacial erratics hauled from nearby farm fields are visible in the hillside woods. At an intersection, where a trail to the left completes the loop around the pine forest, go right up the hill. The hillside to the right of the trail is badly eroded from water reaching it through a large culvert underneath a road ahead. Turning northwest to walk along the left side of a service road, you soon pass restrooms and come to a shelterhouse built in 1972 in memory of Marion Bebb

Howe, the great granddaughter of Governor Bebb.

Stay with the entry road to the right to visit the Pioneer Village and to walk the Serenity Trail. Signs in the village tell of the life and times of Governor Bebb and of the origin of each of the other buildings that have been assembled there. The restoration is said to represent early Butler County at around 1812, when young Bill Bebb was ten years old. Butler County was created when Ohio joined the Union in 1803. Privies, quaintly labeled "womenfolk" and "menfolk," sit between the Gray Cat Tavern and the Bebb house. To the north, beyond the Gary Cabin, is a sign labeling the entrance to the Serenity Trail. To reach it, pass around the left side to the rear of the Gray Cabin. "New" structures are still being added to the village, so your route may need to vary from what is described here.

Before or after hiking the Serenity Trail, walk over to the covered bridge that sits alongside the entry drive. It looks as though at one time it was allowed to carry traffic, but the service road is now routed around it. Steel I-beams help hold it up. Chuckle at the sign that gives the toll for passing through it, dating back to 1828 when it was the Oxford bridge. The design was by Lewis Wernwag, a nineteenth-century bridge architect. This style, with its double arch and flared kingpost truss sets, is said to have been his best design. It may have been built of white pine, perhaps brought from Michigan via the Miami-Erie Canal. The board and batten siding is, of course, new, probably of southern yellow pine. The original roof was probably of split oak shingles, but in restoration cedar was used. Built at its original site three and one-half miles west of Oxford sometime prior to 1873, it was 170-feet long and spanned Indian Creek without a pier. Will the concrete bridges being built today be around 120 years from now? There are a couple of benches beside the bridge, a good place for a trail snack.

Head back through the white oaks and maples to the Serenity Trail. Very shortly after its beginning, the trail drops off the flat land and goes down a set of wooden steps into a ravine. There, it turns left and travels down the wooded ravine for 150 feet. It then crosses the creek to the right and goes up a small ravine for about 75 feet before climbing a set of 34 steps to a white pine planting. Traveling close to the boundary fence for a short way, the trail makes a left-oblique turn into the pines, then emerges near the north boundary of the park. Soon after turning left, the trail again turns left following what looks like an old road. Before reaching a pond, you will see a connecting side trail that drops down the hill to the youth group area below. At the pond, cross the levee on the right (downstream side), looking all the while for frogs, dragonflies, and the like.

The trail follows the edge of the hill, with the pines to the left and the cedars and hardwoods on the rocky hillside to the right. Whoever planted the pines must have had extra seedlings because they are as close as two feet along the edge of the planting. The trail then makes almost a U-turn, heading north back between rows of pines. After about 100 yards, you will reach a hole in the pines and turn 45 degrees to the right into deciduous woods. The trail crosses the dam of another small wildlife pond, then follows the rim of a ravine upstream to soon arrive at the 34 steps for the return to the Pioneer Village. From there, follow the road downhill to your vehicle, bringing an end to your exploration of this unusual, rather remote park that seeks to preserve both the natural and the pioneer history of the Ohio-Indiana border area.

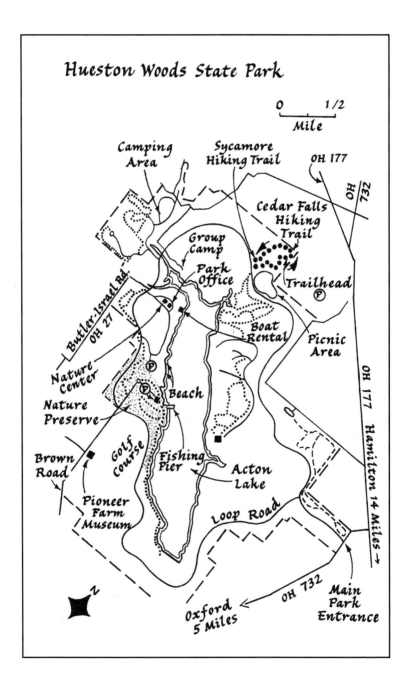

Hueston Woods State Park

0   1/2
Mile

Camping Area
Sycamore Hiking Trail
OH 177
OH 732
Cedar Falls Hiking Trail
Group Camp
Park Office
Trailhead
Butler-Israel Rd.
OH 27
Boat Rental
Picnic Area
Nature Center
OH 177 Hamilton 14 Miles
Nature Preserve
Beach
Brown Road
Golf Course
Fishing Pier
Acton Lake
Pioneer Farm Museum
Loop Road
OH 732
Main Park Entrance
Oxford 5 Miles

Hueston Woods
State Park

Distance: 1½ miles
Accessibility: Trail surface unsuitable for
access by physically challenged.
Facilities: Campground, vacation cabins, lodge, picnic areas,
boating, swimming beach, drinking water, restrooms,
nature center, pioneer farm museum,
sugarbush, and golf course.

Whent Matthew Hueston was serving with "Mad" Anthony Wayne in southwestern Ohio toward the close of the eighteenth century, he thought there was something special about the fertile soil of the area. The land was covered with a magnificent forest of beech, maple, and white oak. After "mustering" out of the army, Hueston began to buy the land in what is now Butler and Preble counties. He cleared much of it to create fertile field for hay and grain, but he preserved a portion of the original forest, as did his descendants.

When the last of the Huestons died in the 1930s, conservationist Morris Taylor of Hamilton purchased much of the land, including the uncut forest, and held it until the state could find the money with which to buy it. Preble County representative Cloyd Acton influenced the legislature to appropriate the money just prior to World War II, and in 1941 it was designated as a state forest. At the close of the war, more land was purchased, and in 1957, Four Mile Creek was impounded to create the 625-acre Acton Lake.

Today, Hueston Woods State Park includes 3,596 acres of land and is a major outdoor recreation destination for thousands of vacationing Ohioans. In spite of its recreational facility development, the climax beech-maple forest that prompted the efforts to protect the area remains intact as a state nature preserve. Visitors to the park

*Water tumbles gently over flat limestone rocks alongside the
Cedar Falls Trail at Hueston Woods State Park.*

often seek the peace and quiet of the trails in this 200-acre tract on
the western side of the lake.

There are other foot trails in the park that hold a different kind
of beauty, however. Here I describe a walk on the Cedar Falls Trail,
which runs alongside a small stream that flows into the lake at its
northeast corner. This walk will bring enjoyment even after frost has
stripped the forest of its coat of many colors.

Access

Hueston Woods State Park is open every day of the year. The main
entrance to the park loop road is on OH 732, 5 miles north of
Oxford. Access to the Cedar Falls hiking trail is from the Sycamore
Grove Picnic Area parking lot, located on the right side of the Loop
Road not quite 3 miles from the main entrance on the east side of
the lake. Stay right at the split in the road that occurs .5 mile inside
the main park entrance.

Trail

The trail originates at the back end of the Sycamore Grove parking lot. It drops from the picnic area and into the stream valley almost immediately, starting out as a crushed gravel trail but soon changing to a natural surface. Turning right, you soon cross over a side stream on a small footbridge. The trail dips up and down in the floodplain and lots of small "wild" trails lead toward the main stream on the left. Passing under buckeyes and sycamores, the earthen trail veers to the right and begins to climb toward the park boundary. A 3½-foot-diameter white oak tree stands at a point where the trail drops again to a low-water crossing. Beyond here, the trail splits—take the right fork. Rising now through beech-maple woodland, the trail parallels the property line about 20 feet to the right.

After 100 yards of climbing the trail reaches a ridge, arcs to the left away from the fenceline, passes some red cedars and white oaks, and soon arrives at the top of a high bluff. There, red oak trees frame the view of the creek below. This is a great place to pause and take a picture.

Continuing on the trail beneath more oaks, cedar, and an occasional basswood, you soon beginning dropping gently toward the stream. Ignore the side trails that lead to the bluff rim. Guard rails once in place along parts of this trail have fallen, the result of weather action on the highly erodible soil. As the trail passes through beech-maple forest, it arcs to the right and then to the left just before reaching the stream. On the late summer day when I last walked this trail, I flushed a great blue heron from the pool of water behind Cedar Falls, now in view on the stream. There was no water coming over the falls on that day, but often when the redbud is in bloom in May, I have seen water tumbling over the layer of limestone slabs that create this falls. The shale bank of the opposite side of the stream adds to the special beauty of this spot. Here, again, is a place to take pictures, turn over a few rocks and explore for invertebrates, crayfish, and salamanders, and hunt for fossils in the rock. Examine and enjoy what you discover, but leave it there to live out its life or be discovered by those who follow.

It is now time to turn downstream along a trail close to the left shore of the creek. There will be times during and following storms when this trail will be impassable, making it necessary to return to the parking lot over the trail that brought you here. During most of the year though, you can follow the streamside trail to a point where you can see the bluff from which you viewed the stream valley. You will pass another falls where water drops over a flat limestone ledge and drops into beds of shales below. The trail moves closer, then more distant from the stream before crossing to the right bank at an obvious opening in the woods.

The flat-rock crossover leads to a trail through the woods, perhaps 12 feet above the elevation of the stream. This is calciphile country, where sweet soils derived from limestone and calcareous shale support plants of all sizes. About 100 feet after entering the trail, there is a side trail to the left that leads to a creekside view of the bluff.

Return to the main trail that now travels on a wide, nearly level floodplain, and continue in a downstream direction beneath such trees as chinquapin oak, black walnut, honey locust, ash, and hackberry. There is some of the bird-dropping-planted alien bush honeysuckle alongside the trail but there are also many native woodland wildflowers present.

After crossing one small creek or former stream channel, the trail reaches a larger one. After a sometimes wet crossing, follow the right bank of this creek downstream to where it joins the main stream at the loop road bridge. A sign at this point identifies the trail and gives the name of the family who have been looking after it as part of the Division of Parks and Recreation's Adopt-a-Trail program.

Turn left to cross the bridge and walk the left shoulder of the road to the Sycamore Grove parking lot. Across the road from its entrance is the trailhead for the Sycamore Trail, a well-marked, short loop trail on the land that lies between the road and the lodge.

As you walk through the parking lot you will find restrooms to the right, and many grills and tables where you can enjoy a meal or a snack under the tall sycamore trees.

Miami Whitewater Forest

Distance: Three trails totaling 3⅔ miles
Accessibility: Access to any trail described here would be
difficult to impossible for physically challenged.
Facilities: Restrooms, drinking water, golf course, bridle trails,
ball fields, bird museum, visitor center, boating, fishing.

Miami Whitewater Forest, at 3,639 acres, is the largest of the regional natural area parks of the Hamilton County Park District. Land purchases for the park, the third in the system, began in 1948, and an 85-acre lake was completed on the site in 1971.

The topography of the area varies from flat, glacial outwash plain to very hilly. The Kansan and Illinoian glaciers reached into the area, but the principal visible effects came from the Wisconsinan glacier, whose advance halted a few miles to the north. Meltwater from that ice sheet cut valleys and deposited outwash in them. The park, most of it upland, is situated between the valleys of the present-day Great Miami and Whitewater Rivers, hence its name.

Underlaid by Ordovician limestone and shales, the soils support rich, mixed mesophytic woodlands. The park district manages the area to provide a great diversity of habitat and is presently working to establish a 100-acre wetland, a 750-acre prairie, and a wetland/prairie native plant seed nursery.

The avifauna of the area is rich and diverse. The park is considered one of Ohio's best areas for birds of prey.

Miami Whitewater Forest provides a wide variety of recreational opportunities for the residents of southwestern Ohio. Among these are three fine hiking trails: the 1¾-mile-long Badlands Trail of challenging difficulty, the 1¼-mile-long Oakleaf Trail of moderate difficulty, and the ⅔-mile-long easy hike on the Tallgrass Prairie Trail. Singly or as a package, these trails provide fine hiking in a natural setting.

As with all parks in the Hamilton County Park District, visitors must either have an annual vehicle parking pass or purchase a daily permit to enter the area.

Access

Located in the northwestern corner of Hamilton County in Harrison, Crosby, and Whitewater townships, Miami Whitewater Forest is easily reached by traveling west on I-74 from I-75 in Cincinnati or from the I-275 outerbelt. Exit I-74 via Exit 3, Dry Fork Road. Go north on Dry Fork Road to West Road, then turn right (east) to cross Dry Fork Creek. There are entrances on both sides of the road just east of the bridge. Turn north (left) to reach the trailheads for the Badlands and Oakleaf trails. Turn south (right) and travel 1.1 miles to reach the Tallgrass Prairie Trail.

Trails

The easiest of the three trails is the Tallgrass Prairie Trail. Although only a small portion of this trail passes through tallgrass prairie, it provides a pleasant and interesting walk during any season of the year. It is especially attractive from July through frost when a procession of tallgrass prairie grasses and forbs come into bloom in the planted prairie area.

The trail passes through young woodland, mature forest, shrubby thicket, oldfield-type meadow, and planted tallgrass prairie. The trailhead sign illustrates some of the small creatures likely to inhabit this diverse habitat, but don't expect to see any of the marvelous miniature mammals of the woods and grasslands, for virtually all move about during the hours of darkness when park visitors have gone home. Focus instead on the invertebrates. In the sunny areas during the summer, look for some of the six species of swallowtail butterflies found in Ohio, and in the fall watch for the monarch collecting nectar en route to its Mexican wintering ground. Also in

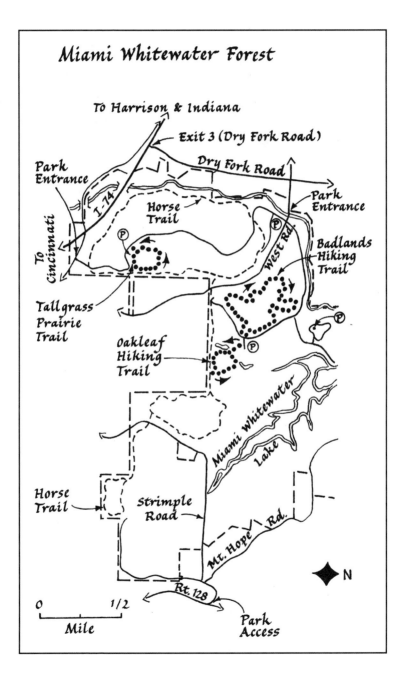

Miami Whitewater Forest

To Harrison & Indiana

Exit 3 (Dry Fork Road)

Dry Fork Road

Park Entrance

I-74

Horse Trail

To Cincinnati

Park Entrance

West Rd.

Badlands Hiking Trail

Tallgrass Prairie Trail

Oakleaf Hiking Trail

Miami Whitewater Lake

Horse Trail

Strimple Road

Mt. Hope Rd.

Rt. 128

Park Access

N

0   1/2

Mile

The even terrain at the entrance to the Oakleaf Trail is deceiving as the path soon drops steeply to travel through rugged, wooded country.

the fall, look for golden garden spiders in the morning mist in the meadow and prairie. In the light shade of the woods see if you can find one or more of the three brown-colored satyr butterflies of the area—the common wood nymph, the northern pearly eye, or the little wood satyr—flitting along the trail. Look for walking sticks, preying mantises, ladybugs, and much more. Thousands of Ohio invertebrates keep the same working hours as hikers and photographers. This is a good place to begin learning more of them and more about them.

The year-long resident birds of this trail are those of suburban backyards—birds of edge, thicket, and open meadow: towhee, goldfinch, downy woodpecker, bluejay, and the like. Listen for the familiar cheer-up, cheer-up of a cardinal and let it cheer up your day.

The trail immediately leaves the parking lot on a grassy path then enters woods on gravel, headed downhill. At about 75 feet from the parking lot, the path splits to form a loop. Head straight ahead to travel in a counterclockwise direction.

The wide woodland trail begins to drop, eventually making a

gentle S-turn as it crosses a draw and heads uphill on crushed stone with water bars to retard erosion. The young regrowth woods includes red cedar now being overtopped by the hardwoods, indicating that cedar is an early field invader after farming is halted. Like much of southwestern Ohio, the shrub layer here contains the alien bush honeysuckle, and garlic-mustard is abundant in the herbaceous layer.

A trail sign announces your arrival at the planted tallgrass prairie for which the trail is named. The sign tells of the loss of Ohio's original prairie and of naturalists' attempts to reconstruct this once important ecosystem. This prairie is said to contain at least 150 species of prairie grasses and forbs and a smaller number of the animals indigenous to the prairie.

Enter the magic of the prairie environment. It was early morning on a mid-August day when I explored this trail. The flowers were simply gorgeous. Here and there a goldfinch bounced in and out to steal a seed for vegetarian energy. Dew was still on the purple coneflowers and, as the sun hit a tall blazingstar, a tiger swallowtail was close behind. Cordgrass stood tall along the trail in the lower, swale-like area, but for most of the reach of the trail through the prairie, big bluestem was hanging over the path. At my feet, yellow partridge pea bloomed, and the drying pods of prairie false-indigo stood out across the landscape. The ambrosialike aroma of milkweed blossoms was in the air. The 180-mm APO macro lens on my camera helped me capture on film closeup vignettes of the prairie plants and the incredible six-legged creatures with which they evolved. A slide of a tall coreopsis blossom examined later showed a crab spider virtually the same color as the flower petals lying in wait for an unsuspecting morsel. Even after frost, when snow has yet to bring the prairie plants to their knees, the seeds and stems against the sky fill a camera's frame or a mind's eye majestically.

It is difficult to move on from here. Perhaps it's the ephemeral nature of the prairie that draws one back to it. The change from just showing green above the earth in May to shoulder high in August seems like magic. Trees are visible year-round but the moment of the prairie seems fleeting; yet, like the trees, long-lived perennials carry on life beneath the surface of the earth six months of the year.

Continuing the counterclockwise loop, the trail heads downhill past some beautiful tall tuliptrees under which is a jumble of vines, including another alien, Japanese honeysuckle. Now on a crushed limestone surface, the trail reaches a bridge with king-post truss sides. Swinging left, it rises from the creek, passing nice shagbark hickories, oaks, and sugar maples before dropping again to a small creek. More tall timber appears as the trail continues to swing right, then passes an open area where there is a sign saying "wildlife management area."

More beautiful tuliptrees and then mixed hardwoods stand above red cedars as the trail drops to the same small creek. There is a small pond off to the right. The trail passes occasional meadow openings and stands of juniper, then turns left along the stream where jewelweed sparkles with dew in late summer. A narrower trail here, it turns left, crossing water bars, as it drops to a raised boardwalk over a small draw. Moving uphill on a few wooden steps, the trail moves gently to the right and rises to the top of a low hill.

Now moving through young woodland that must have been pastureland not too long ago, the trail heads in a left arc toward its junction with the trail to the parking lot.

This short hike starts out very ordinary but becomes very special at the farthest point from the trailhead. Enjoy it year-round, but especially in late July and August.

To reach the Oakleaf Trail, travel north on Park Road, cross West Road, and continue on Park Road to its intersection with Timber Lakes Road. Leave Park Road on Timber Lakes Road, taking it to the Timber Lakes picnic area. There is a restroom close by. The entrance to the Oakleaf Trail is directly across from the restroom door. There is a sign describing the trail and an arrow pointing the way. The 1¼-mile-long trail is described as moderately difficult, requiring an hour to an hour and a half to travel.

This foot trail drops quickly off the high ground, passing through tall hardwoods. On the day I walked it, a wood peewee was calling in the distance. The entry trail down the slope has been rerouted with switchbacks to correct an erosion problem. The new crushed limestone trail is also provided with waterbars. At the onset of the trail, there seems to be an absence of a good understory, but toward the bottom of the slope a more natural layering of small trees, shrubs, and groundcover returns.

Where the trail reaches the lake area, there is a sign that tests your knowledge about oak trees, with upside-down answers. As I read through the quiz, a male Carolina wren called its "teakettle, teakettle, teakettle" song loudly and clearly quite nearby.

There are two "timberlakes." The trail passes over the earthen dam that impounds the one to the right. The headwaters of the one to the left is the outlet stream that comes under the dike from the lake to the right. Above the sill pipe carrying water between the lakes grow spotted jewelweed and tall bellflower in late summer. The lakes appear fairly clean and not overgrown with the algae often seen on park and golf course lakes. Perhaps they get less light in this fairly deep ravine, but they do drain land outside of the park; it is hard to determine what nutrient load the runoff may bring to them.

At the end of the dike, turn right to travel counterclockwise around the loop trail. Soon an interpretive sign tells about the beech trees of the area, admonishing visitors to stroke but not to cut the grey bark of these lovely trees. A four-foot-wide boardwalk carries the trail to the pond shore where a handrail is provided for safe travel. Quiet in August, this pond must resound with the "jug-a-rum" of bull frogs in late May and June.

At the end of the boardwalk, the trail returns to the hillside on gravel. Soon a small stream entering from the left is spanned by a short bridge. Beyond the bridge there is an interpretive sign touting the successful return (on their own) of pileated woodpeckers to the area. Watch and listen for one of these crow-sized, red-crested black and white woodpeckers of the deep forest. They are a joy to see in flight or to watch as they probe a standing dead tree for carpenter ants and other edibles.

Just before the pond turns into a creek, the trail becomes a boardwalk for a short way, then turns to the left up the hill. Climbing perhaps 150 feet in elevation and traveling maybe 150 yards in distance, the trail has well-spaced ties to keep the gravel in place.

Before reaching the top of the hill, the trail turns left, still moving through pleasant mixed mesophytic deciduous forest. Sugar maples make up much of the understory in this deep woods. The trail finally reaches the wide ridgetop, with land falling off to both right and left. There is a large burl on an oak tree here, and a sign talks about the parasitic plant, squawroot, that is common under the oak trees in the area.

As the trail begins to drop, widely spaced waterbars begin to show up on the trail. Where it turns left to return to the valley of the "timberlakes," an interpretive sign appears carrying the story of the incredible nutrients that come from fallen trees. Soon the hiker heads straight down the trail to the water's edge. Before reaching the shore, the trail turns to the left to curve its way back to where it splits at the east end of the dike. First, though, there is a trail to the lake's edge that every hiker will want to take before completing the loop. As I approached the lake, a wood duck lifted off the lake to my right.

Return to the main trail and drop down six railroad tie steps to near lake level. Then climb the hillside to move upstream and rejoin the trail across the dike to the hill and parking lot.

With nothing more exciting than beautiful tall oaks, hickories, beech, and other hardwoods, this trail appears to be lightly used. It is a real jewel, however, to be revisited often.

The same parking lot serves the Badlands Trail, the third and longest of the Miami Whitewater Forest trails. According to the trailhead sign, this trail was named for some unique geological formations that occur along it. Many theories have been proposed as to their origins, but most likely they are large sinkholes made from eroded limestone. Note the "slippery when wet" warning at the trailhead. This hike, the most "natural" and most challenging of the park's trails, is 1¾-miles long and may take up to two hours to negotiate.

Almost immediately after leaving the trailhead sign, the trail drops downhill under tall oaks, hickories, sugar maples, and ash trees on a gravel surface. When it reaches the split that creates the loop, the surface becomes dirt or, often, mud. An arrow on a carsonite post points to the left. The clockwise trail begins by hugging the hillside on the left side of the valley. There appears to be no shrub or understory layer, perhaps due to a present or past deer overgrazing problem. The absence of any lily family members on the hillsides seems to further substantiate this theory.

There is no better way to describe this trail than as "badlands." It negotiates the most unusual natural landscape that I have ever traveled in Ohio—a collection of pockets and knolls, narrow ridges and gullies, that is hard to believe. You will negotiate short railroad tie steps with handrails, longer rises with waterbars, here and there a piece of boardwalk, a number of bridges, including one twenty-five feet long, and more. You will witness vegetative cover from mature forest to lone, white oak "wolf trees" and areas covered with sassafras and dogwood, indicating acid substrate. The vegetation is, however, mostly red cedars growing on the thin soil derived from Ordovician bedrock.

Much of the time while negotiating this trail I had no idea where I was. After many twists and turns, ups and downs, and creek and gully crossings, I descended a slope with railroad-tie waterbars, yet still so slippery that I held onto the pawpaw trees on the right before reaching the eighteen-foot-long bridge over a dry streambed. After that, I climbed a steep hillside with ten railroad ties serving as steps of a fashion. As the trail began to level out, suddenly I ended up back at the junction where I had entered the badlands. A turn to the left and I was back on crushed limestone, scurrying across the thirty railroad-tie waterbars on the short trail back to the parking lot.

This is a rugged, walking-stick ramble in a class by itself. Don't try it alone, like I did, but do try it: you'll like it.

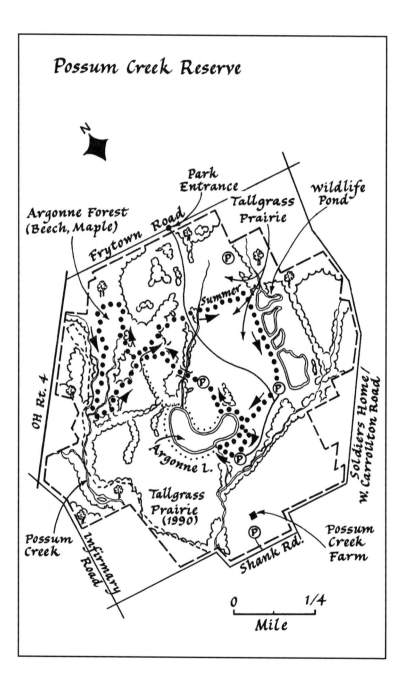

Possum Creek Reserve

Possum Creek Reserve

Distance: 2½ miles
Accessibility: Natural surface trails might be
soggy in some seasons but access by physically
challenged possible in most areas with assistance.
Facilities: Farmstead, fishing pond, picnic tables
and shelters, restrooms, drinking water, wildlife
observation blind, bridle trails, planted prairie.

Most of the 518-acre Possum Creek Reserve has not seen a farmstead, plow, or cow for a long time. Bush and Japanese honeysuckle, multiflora rose, privet, and other plants kept neatly "in their places" when the land was farmed have spread like wildfire across the abandoned fields. The terrain is flat and poorly drained, having been badly abused. Much of it had its rich topsoil scraped off and sold. Every now and again a granite boulder will stare at you to remind you how the land got so flat— not too long ago in geologic time a glacier passed this way. Yet, it is an exciting place to walk. If you like to "read the land" as I do, there is a new "book" around every corner. In the almost two decades since the park district acquired the land, it has given Possum Creek a personality all its own. It's one I think you will find worth getting to know.

Access

Possum Creek Reserve is situated in Jefferson Township in Montgomery County, no further than 6 miles from downtown Dayton. It lies east of OH 4 on Frytown Road. The entrance is less than .5 mile from the state highway. It is open without charge from 8 A.M. until dusk every day except Christmas and New Year's Day.

Trail

Unlike most places in this book, there appear to be no named trails at Possum Creek. The route taken here has been chosen because it challenges the hiker to use his or her powers of observation to figure out what different areas of the reserve looked like in the past and how it might look in the future.

After entering the reserve from the north, drive to the furthest parking lot. Walk toward Argonne Lake on the trail at the right end of the lot. You will be traveling through an old field full of summer wildflowers that butterflies love. Take a right turn at the shore and follow the trail around the end of the lake, passing two side trails and a restroom and picnic facilities on the way. When you reach a third side trail going straight north, take it. This path was probably an old road or driveway. An alley of bush honeysuckle likely send its sweet scent forth for miles on a damp night when it is in bloom.

On the far side of the picnic area and parking lot to the left, under the maples, is a bulletin board. Beyond it, and leaving from the northwest corner of the lot, is a trail that might not be on your park district map. Shortly down that trail, you cross a fairly new bridge over the small stream that feeds Argonne Lake. Proceeding past old field and thicket and an occasional large tree, the trail makes an S-curve, turning sharply left, then right, before reaching a "T" at an area with large beech and sugar maple trees.

Turn left, then go straight ahead, ignoring a trail headed south to the lake. On the right, there is a mowed area with picnic tables and a group camping area also called "Argonne." Just beyond that facility, turn right through a wet area with lots of young trees. An interpretive sign at a "T" ahead provides a clue about the origins of the stone wall over by the creek. Turn right at the next "T". Beyond, where only large old trees are visible now, was once an amusement park called Argonne Forest created by World War I veterans who had fought together in France. In the thirties and early forties, a target range, swimming pool, ball diamond, dance hall, auto race track, and vacation cabins stood there. Old streetcars were brought in as diners. Can you picture where things might have stood? If the

The three-lobed coneflower is one of several plant species of the prairie and woodland border that is commonly called "black-eyed Susan."

old beech, maple, and oak trees could talk, what stories of war, mystery, and romance they might tell.

After a turn around "the forest," do not close the loop but continue on the trail to the south, paralleling the east branch of Possum Creek. After ¼ mile of traveling through young tree and thicket, the trail turns left across two small streams and goes past cedar glades, heading northeast back toward the Argonne Group Camping area. At that point, turn right (east) and follow the trail as it jogs left, then right, then left again past the northern end of "honeysuckle alley," soon to reach the entry road.

In 1980, park district employees started planting the field across the road with native prairie grasses and forbs. The park now boasts of one of the largest planted prairies in Ohio. It is big enough to take on the visual character of "a sea of grass." Judging from the presence of some old burr oak trees in the park, it is conceivable that there may have been some prairie in the area prior to settlement. If not here, certainly nearby.

To the lover of the prairie, the next ¼ mile brings pure joy. An interpretive sign tells the story of the reestablishment of the prairie, but only a good wildflower guidebook will teach you what to call these long-lived, deep-rooted perennials of the prairie. John Madson's *Where the Sky Began* will entice you with the "prairie fever."

Beyond the prairie, the trail breaks through an old fencerow; turn right (south) to walk alongside a wildlife pond and more fishing lakes. To the south, ⅓ mile, is a parking lot and restrooms. From there, either walk the entry road to your car or take the trail across the road to the east end of Argonne Lake, where a trail to the left leads to the lot.

To see the prairie flowers, a summer walk is in order, but to read the landscape of the Argonne Forest will require a trek after the leaves have fallen.

Siegenthaler Esker State Nature Preserve

Distance: 1½ miles
Accessibility: Occasional steep slope and grass trail surface make access for physically challenged nearly impossible except perhaps with a strong aide.
Facilities: None

Rising above the surface of this gently rolling western Ohio land, like disjointed sections of an earthen flood levee, stand two grass-covered gravel ridges. Geologists call them "eskers." They are not "Indian earthworks" or the work of some mad landscape architect but rather deposits of sand and gravel left there by the melting Wisconsinan glacier perhaps 11,000 years ago.

When that glacier, which covered this part of Ohio, was melting, a meltwater stream tunnelled through the ice. Slowed down by the level surface, it dropped its load of sand and gravel in the bottom of the tunnel in sorted layers, depending upon the speed of the moving water. After the glacier melted, a long narrow ridge of gravel, an esker, remained behind. Here, though not always the case, this sinuous esker has a north-south orientation. The water in the ice-walled stream was probably moving toward the broad valley of today's Great Miami River. A smaller, less well defined esker lies to the west of the main esker, and several kames, a conical type of water-deposited glacial landform, occur to the northwest. Several kettle lakes occur nearby, which, together with the ground moraine, kames, and esker, provide a good review of glacially produced landforms.

At the time of settlement, many kames and eskers could be found across central and southwestern Ohio, but in the interval since, most have been destroyed. In some places, the eskers carry roads or have houses built on them. Most kames and eskers have been used

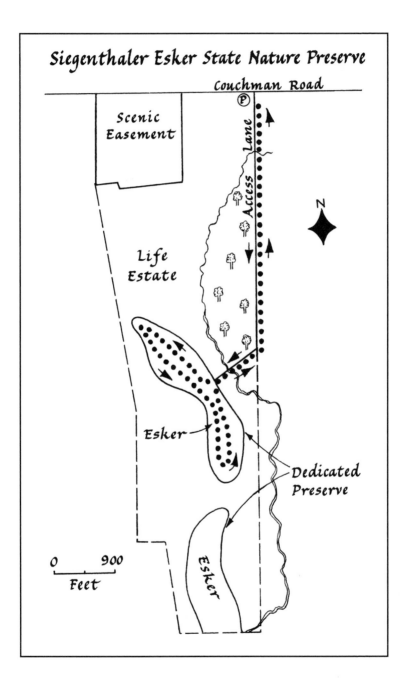

Siegenthaler Esker State Nature Preserve

as ready sources of sand and gravel. It is much easier to obtain this construction material from where it is already piled up and reasonably dry than from beneath the surface of a gravel- (and water-) filled glacial outwash valley.

In 1978, Vaughn and Frieda Siegenthaler, wishing to see this unique glacial landform saved for future generations to know and study, made a generous donation to the state of Ohio of a 37-acre tract that contains most of the esker. The Division of Natural Areas and Preserves manages it in such a way as to keep most of the woody vegetation, except for burr oak trees, off the esker. This is done in the belief that the condition that results will replicate that natural vegetation found at the time of settlement. This plan requires lots of hand cutting and the occasional use of fire and herbicides. Since 1992, the preserve has been open to the public. The south esker extends beyond the preserve boundary and is off limits to hikers, but officials of the Division of Natural Areas and Preserves hope that it can someday be included in the preserve.

Access

Dedicated as an interpretive preserve in the state natural area system, Siegenthaler Esker is located in Harrison Township in northern Champaign County. It is reached by taking OH 245 west from West Liberty not quite 5 miles to Church Road, then turning south (left) 1 mile to Couchman Road. Head west (right) on Couchman Road about .5 mile to a small parking pulloff on the south (left) side of the road. Pets are not permitted.

Trail

Since bedrock from here north to the Lake Erie basin is mostly limestone or dolomite, the rocky material of the kames, eskers, and moraines of the area is probably at least 65 percent calcareous. The remainder is rock of igneous origin, tumbled here from the Canadian shield by the glaciers: rounded pieces of granite, gneiss, and the like, mostly small but occasionally large (the boulders we call glacial erratics). The alkalinity of the parent material for the soil is reflected in the woody vegetation throughout the preserve.

Nodding onion, a common plant of the midwest prairies, thrives on the well-drained soils of Siegenthaler Esker.

Under the terms of the land gift, the field to the right of the entry lane is still used by the Siegenthaler family for grazing cattle. After ½ mile of traveling on the lane, where it passes some old "wolf trees" and some young woods, the trail turns right to dip through a low area to the north esker. (One morning when I walked the trail, there was a large doe grazing in the lane far out in front of me.) Upon reaching the esker, climb to the top to get a good view of the land. You can see some of the material that makes up the esker in a bare spot in the trail.

Because eskers are composed of mostly gravel and stand above the surrounding land, they drain and dry out rapidly. They are thus good habitat for dry prairie plants, and among the first to be seen on the top of the moraine on a midsummer's day are wild petunia, false boneset, and lots of nodding onion. The deep-rooted burr oaks, with their thick bark that protects them from the occasional wildfire, are frequently found on the tops of west central Ohio eskers.

Since rainwater drains quickly out of an esker, there are frequently small wetlands at their bases. Such is the case here, and the uncommon tiger salamander has been reported in it. Because of the calcareous nature of the rock in the esker, adjacent wetlands are sometimes fens. (A good example of such an esker-associated fen can be seen on both sides of OH 4 in northeastern Clark County, just north of Baldwin Lane.)

From here, the trail is less defined. Explore the north esker, eat a trail snack, and watch for birds and butterflies (yes, some species do nectar on nodding onion). Male black swallowtail butterflies are fond of hilltops, so look especially for them. Their larvae feed on members of the *Umbellifera* family such as the alien Queen Anne's lace, so they should be in the area. On a late summer afternoon when I was here, I saw several monarch butterflies with their characteristic strong fly-and-glide flight pattern come across the esker.

Speculate on what the area may have looked like before road, fences, ditches, and buildings. Can you visualize a prairie swale to the west? Perhaps by late summer, bison were migrating north with the maturing of warm-season grasses and were grazing close to the horizon here. The loose gravel of the esker might have been home to thirteen-lined ground squirrels and an easy place for a badger to dig a dry den in which to raise a family fed on them. Return the way you came.

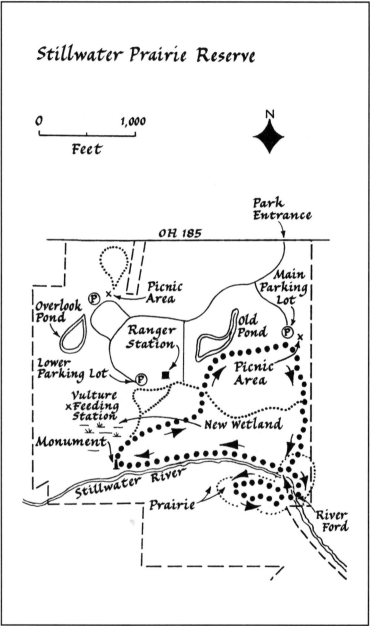

Stillwater Prairie Reserve

0   1,000

Feet

N

Park
Entrance

OH 185

Main
Parking
Lot

Picnic
Area

Overlook
Pond

Old
Pond

Ranger
Station

Picnic
Area

Lower
Parking Lot

Vulture
Feeding
Station

New Wetland

Monument

Stillwater River

Prairie

River
Ford

Stillwater Prairie Reserve

Distance: 1¼ miles
Accessibility: fine gravel, boardwalk, or blacktop
surface on most of this trail make access by physically
challenged possible with some assistance.
Facilities: Restrooms, drinking water, picnic tables,
fishing lakes, a planted prairie,
and a man-made wetland.

Western Ohio's Stillwater River meanders its way east from near the Ohio-Indiana border, passing over progressively older Silurian-age bedrock before it makes an abrupt turn south to join the Great Miami River at Dayton. In most places, the casual observer cannot see the rock layers beneath the surface of the river. Where Stillwater Prairie Reserve spans the river in Miami County, however, the bedrock is obvious. Here the river carved its way through the layers of limestone; a bare limestone ledge lines one bank.

Like other places in the Midwest where there is thin soil above dolomite and limestone, prairie plants flourish in this preserve. Partridge pea, nodding onion, and harebell hold on to life in the pockets of soil in the bedrock on the north side of the river. On the south side, where the bedrock is covered with glacial outwash, prairie dock, purple coneflower, big bluestem, and dozens of other prairie grasses and forbs occur. Like grasslands elsewhere in Ohio, they are thought to be remnants of the prairie that extended further east during a postglacial period when the climate was warmer and dryer. They remained after cool weather returned because of favorable soil and water situations.

The Miami County Park District acquired the original 217-acre tract of this preserve in 1977 to protect this unusual vegetation.

In addition to the riverside prairie, the park includes a mature forest of oak and hickory on the morainal upland. A well-designed and -maintained trail system helps the visitor know and enjoy the varied habitats of the very special reserve. The "getting there," as well as what you see when you arrive, can be memorable since to reach the tallgrass prairie on the south side of the river you must wade the river.

Seventy-four miles of the Stillwater River and its principal tributary, Greeneville Creek, have been designated as a state scenic river by the Ohio Department of Natural Resources. The reach through this reserve is certainly one of the most scenic.

Access

Newberry Township in the northwest corner of Miami County is the site of this park. It is easily reached by traveling 1.7 miles west from OH 48 on OH 185. The entrance is on the south (left) side of the road, and the park is open year-round until one-half hour after sunset.

Trail

After entering the park, make a left turn past the flagpole and park at the main picnic area. The only restrooms and drinking water are located here. To begin hiking, cross the picnic area to the bulletin board and head into the woods on the wide gravel trail. The strip of woods is narrow but contains some nice oaks, hickories, maple, and other hardwoods. Bush honeysuckle has found its way into the understory, but the spring flora is still quite abundant. About 200 yards beyond the trailhead bulletin board, there is a bridge across a small wash; just beyond is a split in the trail.

Continue on the left trail, and in another 200 yards, the trail begins dropping to the river. At a juncture in the trail, a sign introduces the Stillwater prairie and points left to a narrow board-walk that you take to the river's edge. Before reaching the river, the trail passes through an old field area being managed to increase prairie. Look for some of the plants of the drier prairie along the upper edge of the exposed rock.

When sunshine follows a mid-summer shower, giant swallowtails can occasionally be seen "puddling" in the water that collects in the depression in the limestone ledge beside the Stillwater River.

If the river level is normal and the water not too cold, wade to the other side and walk the loop trail through the tallgrass prairie there. A brochure about the prairie should be available in a dispensing box on the north side of the river. The prairie plants are at their best from mid-July to late August, but it is worth the trip even if all you see is the tall big bluestem, visible any time in the fall until the snow knocks it down.

After returning to the north shore and the boardwalk, take the left fork at the trail intersection to head upriver under the tall trees of the riverine forest. Pause long enough to listen to the water rushing over the limestone ledges in the river. Then continue along the shaded trail for ½ mile to the glacial erratic where the state scenic river plaque is mounted. You will have crossed numerous bridges over water seeping from the bottom of the moraine deposits to the north.

A turn to the right takes you into the open to cross a wet meadow on an elevated section of trail. To the left is a shallow wetland created in 1993. An observation tower overlooking the wetland is soon to be constructed. To the far left is a platform on which dead livestock from neighboring farmers are occasionally placed to feed the summertime turkey vulture population. Up the hill to the northwest is a small pond open to fishing by the park visitor. No license is necessary to fish. There are a few picnic tables at the edge of the woods just beyond and a short boardwalk trail through that woods.

Cross the open field at an angle to the right. You will see an old farm homestead, springhouse, barn, and wetland off to the left. The trail crosses a small bridge, then winds its way uphill. Take a left at the next intersection to continue uphill, then, at the next "T" junction, turn right. The mowed trail passes an older pond that was on the property when it was purchased. It, too, is open for fishing without a licence. Some fishermen prefer the old one, others, the new. From the old pond, the trail goes east through a hole in an old fencerow, then travels between meadows kept open for wildlife habitat diversity before returning to the parking lot.

Stillwater Prairie Reserve offers lots to see all year long, but in late July and August when the prairie plants are in bloom, the river is right for wading, and the butterflies are mesmerized by the blooming joe-pye weed and milkweed, it's hard to imagine a better place for a naturalist, a would-be naturalist, or a nature lover to explore.

Taylorsville Reserve

Distance: 2¼ miles
Accessibility: A rocky talus slope makes this trail
impassable for physically challenged.
Facilities: Restrooms, picnic tables and shelters,
drinking water, fishing, group campsite, Buckeye Trail,
wildlife observation blind,
and sledding hill.

After a major flood inundated much of downtown Dayton in 1913, the city fathers set about to make certain such a tragedy could never recur. In 1915, the Miami Conservancy District was formed, and by 1922, five flood control dams had been built on the Great Miami River and its tributaries. This system of "dry dams," which holds back water only during a flood, is said to have been the first comprehensive approach to flood prevention through reservoir use in the United States. Taylorsville Dam was constructed on the main stem of the Great Miami River, eight miles north of downtown Dayton.

Access

Taylorsville Reserve is a major nature-oriented recreation area operated by the Park District of Dayton-Montgomery County on land under lease from the Conservancy District. The community of Taylorsville, for which the reservoir is named, lies just east of the Great Miami River about 1 mile south of the dam in Miami County's Wayne Township.

To reach the trails on the side of the river, travel north from I-70 2 miles on OH 202 to US 40 at Phonton (named for the major long-distance telephone exchange that at one time operated around the clock in the brick building on the southwest corner of the intersection). Turn left (west) on US 40. About 1 mile west of Phonton, you will see where the National Road (US 40) once went straight ahead to cross the river but now turns left (south). Travel 1 mile past the left turn and you will find a park entrance and picnic area on the right (west) side. The trailhead is located here.

Trail

Head downhill from the northwestern corner of the parking lot. The trail passes an information shelter where maps are available. To the left is a Great Depression-era picnic shelter built by the Civilian Conservation Corps (CCC), Co. 3511, Camp SP20, in 1936. It was restored by members of the CCC Veterans chapter 122 of Dayton in 1989. It is a fine example of the work those "boys" did in local and national parks across the land so many years ago.

Take the trail to the right just opposite the shelterhouse. There is a trail map posted there and a self-guiding trail folder keyed to numbered posts on the short loop trail near the shelterhouse. The grass ends as the trail drops down steps to cross the first of many small streams that run to the river from the east. After passing a trail coming in from the left, the trail along the hillside passes a place where a massive rockslide occurred in 1984, dropping 375 tons of overhanging limestone. The notch in the 425- to 450-year-old limestone cliff above shows where the massive slump-blocks along the trail originated. Glacial erratics, hauled from farm fields above, rest on the rubble of the bedrock talus slope. The trail is moving through a fine woods with tall timber, a nice understory and shrub layer, and apparently a diverse forest floor flora.

For almost a mile, the trail will go due north, traveling mostly below the Silurian dolomite rock wall to the right but sometimes rising onto glacial till close to road level, where there is an occasional picnic table. It moves through sections of younger woods, past pine plantings, and across bridges, old and new, that span the streams coming from the cliff. The trail construction work of the CCC is evident all along this trail.

The sounds of trucks on nearby US 40, trains on the track across the river, and airplanes overhead making their approach to

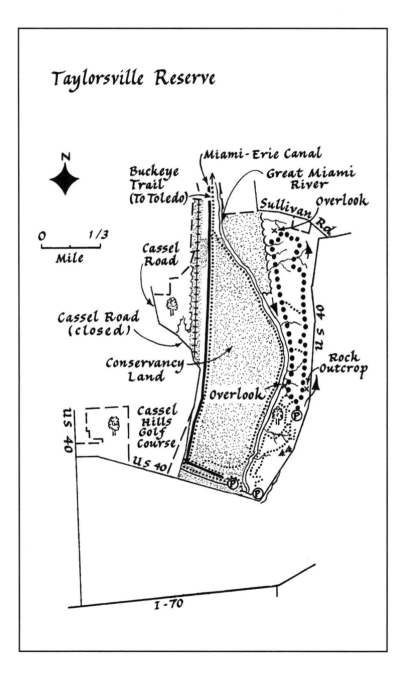

Taylorsville Reserve

Originally built by members of the depression-era Civilian Conservation Corps in 1936, this stone shelter was restored by Corps veterans in 1989.

Cox International Airport are always present.

At the second picnic table, there is a side trail to the left to the river. Ignore it and continue north. Beyond two stream crossings, there is a "wild" trail out to the road and another down the hill, both to be passed by. After traveling through an area with beautiful oaks, the trail rises to where another "wild" trail leads to the road. Just beyond, where a "trail resting" sign blocks an old path, the trail angles to the left. In the woods to the left are some old pine trees. These are probably red pine, a species once used extensively for reforestation and possibly planted by the CCC.

The trail drops into a gully that was evidently heavily eroded when purchased. There are red cedars here and there, more planted pines, and a bench on which to rest. Turning north uphill through young mixed hardwoods, the trail soon comes within sight of the cleared right-of-way through which US 40 descended to the river before construction of the dam.

At the right-of-way, which now carries two powerlines, the trail turns left. The usual oldfield and prairie species typical of western Ohio powerline right-of-ways bloom here through July, August, and September.

Exit the right-of-way to the right into the woods, pass another "trail closed—do not enter—this area is resting" sign, then follow the trail as it twists and turns downhill to eventually reach an overlook. From here, the farm fields of the floodplain behind the dam are visible in the valley to the west. Leaving the overlook, the trail turns back toward the right-of-way on a slippery slope.

A "hiker" emblem posted on the far side of the right-of-way identifies the entrance to the return trail. Railroad ties across the trail help level the trail as it drops toward the base of the slope. With a creek on the right, follow the now-gravel trail as it continues downhill. At a trail intersection, follow the trail to the left as it moves down the valley. The farm fields between here and the river are not a part of the reserve, having been retained by the Conservancy District and leased for agricultural production. Sewage-treatment-plant sludge from Tipp City upriver is applied to these fields as fertilizer.

Now following what looks to be an old road, you will cross several small streams on wooden bridges and pass the entrances to three trails, all going off to the left, before reaching the river's edge. This is a distance of about ½ mile since reaching the road. Notice that this old river-valley road was not located close to the river where it could often be underwater and would use up good cropland, but rather was situated a short ways up the hillside where it would not be vulnerable to flooding.

As you approach the river's edge through typical riverine forest, the valley narrows with the talus slope now almost at river's edge. Side trails for fishermen and just plain river watchers soon increase in frequency. Trails spur off to the left, upslope to the picnic areas you passed earlier, and the streams you had crossed at the base of the cliffs above find their outlets to the river along here. Some are bridged while other require only a long step or two.

You will soon come to the mouth of the stream downslope from the falls that you passed near the beginning of your hike. The limestone rubble is deep, but, though there is no bridge, it is not difficult to get across. Beyond, there is an overlook and a set of stone steps coming down from the picnic area. Either take these steps to the left back to the picnic area, or ignore them and return to the river's edge where trees arching out over the river provide picture-taking opportunities. Here, the trail would surely be underwater during and following any storm.

After crossing one more rocky side stream, you will leave the valley on a wooden staircase that leads to an overlook. A gravel path continues uphill, passing side trails both to the right and left before reaching the picnic shelter and parking lot.

Indian Creek
Watershed

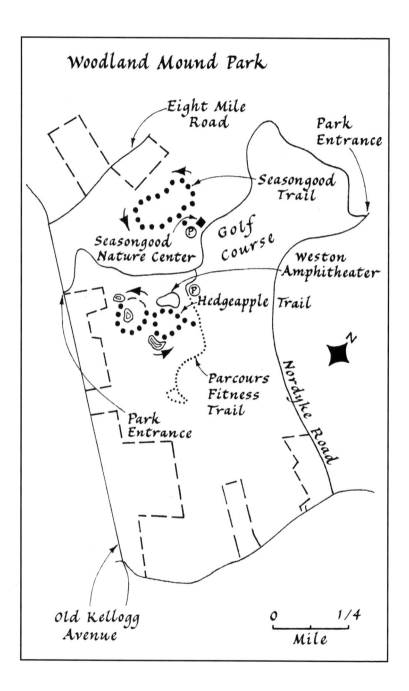

Woodland Mound Park

Woodland Mound Park

Distance: 1½ miles
Accessibility: Hilly terrain and trail surface
conditions make travel on these trails
impossible by physically challenged.
Facilities: Drinking water, restrooms, picnic tables and
shelters, golf course, nature center, frisbee golf.

Although a park in Anderson Township was first proposed in a 1934 park district master plan, it was 1974 before land acquisition began for Woodland Mound Park. With 926 acres, it is fifth in size among the Hamilton County parks. Located north of the Ohio River approximately 17 miles east of Cincinnati in eastern Hamilton and western Clermont counties, it is roughly bounded by the river on the south, Eight Mile Creek on the west, Hopper Hill Road on the west, and Green Road on the north. The rugged and diverse topography has nearly all been heavily affected by the presence of humankind. Though developed as a multirecreational park, most of the area is being allowed to revert through succession to natural landscape. Among the facilities that have been developed are two nature trails that total about 1½ miles in length.

Central to the park is the beautiful Seasongood Nature Center, made possible through the generous legacy of Murray and Agnes Seasongood. Begin exploring this lesser-known regional park by first visiting this unusual facility. One trail originates there; the other, from a parking lot about .2 mile away.

Access

Straddling the Hamilton-Clermont county line southeast of Cincinnati, Woodland Mound Park is reached by exiting I-275 to the west on OH 125, Beechmont Avenue, then turning left (south) on Nordyke Road. The entrance to the main area of the park is on the right just after passing the golf course and Sweetwine Lodge entrance on the left.

Like all other facilities of the Hamilton County Park District, possession of a $3.00 annual vehicle permit or payment of a $1.00 daily vehicle entry fee is required for admittance. A map of the area and cards describing the Seasongood and Hedgeapple trails can be obtained at the nature center or by calling (513) 521-PARK.

Trails

Enjoy the metal sculpture on the grounds outside the Seasongood Nature Center and the exhibits inside, then begin your exploration of the outdoor environment of Woodland Mound Park by hiking the ½-mile Seasongood Nature Trail.

The gravel path that descends the hillside to the trailhead originates at the northeast corner of the nature center. At the trailhead, located just inside the woods, a sign describes the trail as one that passes through a variety of habitats as it winds its way along a ridge high above the Ohio River. Lists of wildlife and wildflower species that might be seen are accompanied by a nice Mary Louise Holt illustration.

The Seasongood Trail is essentially a loop trail, splitting to begin one-way travel not far beyond the trailhead. Because it moves near the edges of field and forest, it is a good hike for watching birds that are edge dwellers. Many of these are the same year-round residents that abide in our neighborhoods, including the sleek Cooper's hawk that sometimes preys on birds congregated near feeders. This habitat is the more natural home for towhees, cardinals, bluejays, and Carolina wrens than are urban neighborhoods. The butterflies that are "hilltoppers," such as the eastern black swallowtail, can be found in the high meadows of the park.

The bedrock of the area is of Ordovician origin—calcareous limestones and shales. Unlike other parts of Hamilton County, the Wisconsinan glacier did not reach this area, so the soils are of Illinoian origin, highly leached and eroded. The vegetation of the area reflects

*A family of great horned owls and a white-tailed deer fawn,
depicted in the sculpture at the entrance to the Seasongood Nature Center,
might quite likely be seen or heard along the trail.*

the limestone origin of the substrate, with the presence of trees that do
well in alkaline situations such as hackberry and red cedar.

From the trailhead sign, descend steps, then cross a small ravine
on fill over a culvert, heading toward an area of regrowth woodland.
Turning gently to the left and passing a "litterbugs learn new tricks"
sign, the broad, crushed gravel trail winds its way gently uphill. It
is a pretty good climb to the point where the return trail enters from
the left and you get to test your knowledge on an "American robin
quiz" sign.

Continuing uphill and following the trail in a counterclockwise
manner as it arcs toward the summit, you will soon find a convenient
bench upon which to sit and rest. To the left is open field habitat, and
a sign tells of the kinds of creatures you might observe in this area.

The open meadow at the entrance to Woodland Mound Park's Seasongood Trail is a good place to observe nectaring butterflies on a sunny summer day.

About 80 feet further down the trail, a sign tells about owl camouflage and their adaptation of silent flight, which facilitates their hunting in woods and fields. Four species of owls are seen (or heard) in the park: the migrant saw-whet that might be spotted hiding in cedar trees or grape vines in the winter, and the year-round resident screech, barred, and great horned owls. Since they are active during the hours when the park is closed, they are seldom seen by the visitor when trees are in leaf; but hikers with a keen eye can occasionally spot them roosting close to the trunk during the rest of the year. During breeding season, they sometimes call during the daytime; at other times of the year naturalists are often able to "call them up" during the crepuscular hours of the day.

Now on nearly level ground, the trail turns to head almost due south through a stand of hickories and other hardwoods. "Is there fungus among us?" is the topic of a well-illustrated trailside interpretive sign to the left of the trail.

The once-extirpated pileated woodpecker is the subject of the next sign, this time on the right. Large chips of wood on the ground below oblong holes in decaying trees give away the presence of this crow-sized member of the *Picadae* family. It has been seeking its favorite food, the carpenter ant. A ringing, irregular "kik-kik-kikkik-kikkik" call rising and falling in pitch from a tree-top perch helps identify this majestic "cock-of-the-woods." In flight, the red cockade and the flashing white of the underside of the wings cinch the identification.

The forest thins, and alien Japanese honeysuckle covers much of the ground as the trail curves left and begins to descend over a couple dozen widely spaced steps with handrails on the right at appropriate spots. Another alien weed, garlic mustard, seems to be thriving along this fairly open section of the trail.

After descending, the trail begins rising through an open area via a half-dozen steps. A bench provides a place to "huff-and-puff." At a red cedar a few more steps up the trail, "homes for wildlife" are discussed on another interpretive sign. Though none are visible from this point, artificial nesting structures are described.

Moving through the young deciduous woods, the careful observer will see that the area's first woody invaders after the land was removed from agricultural use were red cedars. Now being overtopped by hardwoods, these prickly-needled evergreens reveal the calcareous nature of the Ordovician bedrock-derived soils.

The seldom-seen flying squirrel is the topic of the next interpretive station along the still rising, open woodland trail. Highly secretive and strictly nocturnal, the furred gliding rodent is known to appear in the area.

Just before the trail makes a 180-degree turn toward the trail confluence, there is an ash tree covered with poison ivy. The three-leaved climber has reached about 35 feet above the ground. Though best avoided by humans, poison ivy provides a splash of red to the trailside when its leaves turn in the autumn, and birds enjoy its white berries as winter bears down on Ohio.

A right turn at the "robin quiz" sign heads the hiker back toward the nature center. The interpretive signs with their artwork by Mary Louise Holt and Sally Sisson Anderson have added much to the enjoyment of this trail.

Next, explore the Hedgeapple Trail on a slope lower down the hillside overlooking the mighty Ohio River. To reach the trailhead, walk or drive to the Weston Amphitheater parking lot further down the park road. Three trails originate here: one to the right that leads to the amphitheater, one to the far left that goes to a Parcours fitness trail, and, slightly to the left of the amphitheater trail, the mile-long Hedgeapple hiking trail. A trailhead sign tells of the cultural and natural history of the area and of the origin of the trail name.

The trail is named for the hedgeapple or osage orange tree that grows in abundance in this area. Neither related to the orange or the apple, this native to the south central region of the country became widespread throughout the East when, in the nineteenth century, it was planted as a "living fence" or hedgerow. The Osage Indians made bows from its heavy bright orange wood, and a yellow dye can be extracted from its roots, used to dye cloth and baskets.

Heading downslope between large bush honeysuckle trees, the trail soon splits. From this point, the trail configuration is that of a figure eight, although when I walked it in the summer of 1992, one side of the further loop was closed. Perhaps it's because of my right-handedness, but once again I opt for a counterclockwise trek, taking the path to the right.

From the split, the crushed stone trail winds its way downslope between the osage orange, bush honeysuckle, red maple, and other hardwood species. There are openings filled with old field species scattered along the way. In some of the wooded areas, the biennial pest species, garlic mustard, has a firmly established hold on the herb layer along the trail.

At an intersection under, appropriately, a hedgeapple tree, signs point left to the return trail and to the right and ahead to the pond. Go straight ahead. There are multiflora rose and red cedar in the mix in this regrowth woodland area, and chinquapin oak, the calciphile of the beech family, shows up here and there. As the gravel trail continues downhill, widely spaced, treated timbers prevent rapid erosion. Side trails insufficient for human travel reveal the presence of a sizable deer population that probably moves out of the bush to the lawn areas to feed after the gate is shut.

As the trail levels out and arcs to the right, on the right there is a split rail fence at the head of small ravine and, beyond, a man-made pond. Probably used as a breeding place by a succession of amphibians in the spring, it was being used as a hunting ground by dragonflies on the August day when I passed by.

The trail follows the top of the earthen dike, then drops on steps with handrails to cross the outflow from the pond on a small wooden bridge. A few steps beyond lies another pond, this one to the left of the trail. The first interpretive sign on this trail relates to the great variety of life that can be found here and includes the Leonardo Da Vinci quotation from the sixteenth century, "In nature's invention, nothing is lacking, nothing is superfluous. The natural world is ours to enjoy, to be curious about, and to know." A midland painted turtle was basking in the open water of the cattail ringed-pond on the evening of my visit.

Beyond this point, the trail was closed when I was here. If reopened, it will lead you via a mowed grass path alongside open fields where a sequence of summer wildflowers will dazzle you, and at certain times of the year, it will provide a view of the Ohio River valley. An interpretive sign has an illustration of everybody's favorite flower of the field, the black-eyed Susan, and of a hognose snake, the toad-eating comic of the snake world. The trail winds its way uphill through cedar thicket and meadow. When the amphitheater comes into view, it hangs a right to reenter the world of thicket and successional woodland. At the trail intersection, go straight across to complete the figure eight. (If the western half of the lower loop is still closed, return to the intersection on the path you came in on and enjoy the sights of nature from the reverse viewpoint. This exercise often yields surprises—things missed because you came from the other direction and sights and objects overlooked on the first pass.)

Beyond a long reach among osage orange, black locust, and bush honeysuckle, the trail turns sharply left. There is a large nesting box overhead, and beyond that, to the right of the trail, lies a nice vernal pond. Some impervious strata of bedrock or clay must lie beneath the surface here, creating this catchment. Presumably it is fed by run-off, filled during the critical spring breeding season of northern temperate zone amphibians and insects.

A couple dozen steps constructed of half-length railroad ties bring the walker up the steep part of the hillside. As the grade lessens, the trail swings left to "T" with the entry trail, which returns the hiker to the trailhead and parking lot.

Little Miami River Watershed

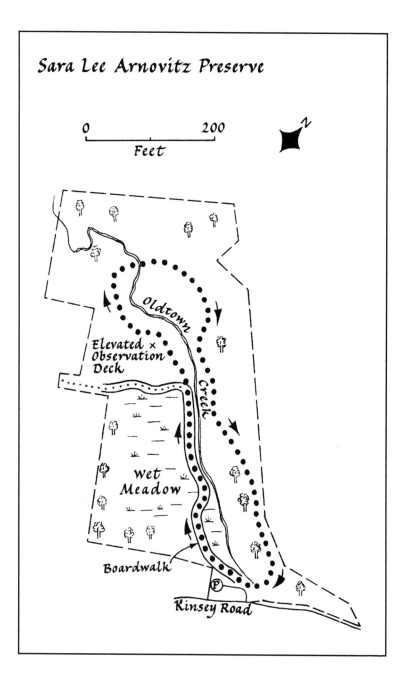

Sara Lee Arnovitz Preserve

Distance: ½ mile
Accessibility: Steps leading into the preserve and steep terrain
make this trail inaccessible to physically challenged.
Facilities: None

On the night of March 9, 1768, the southwestern Ohio sky suddenly lit up as a brilliant meteor streaked across the heavens. At about the same time, the silence was broken by the sound of a newborn crying near a Shawnee village not more than ¼ mile from the location of Arnovitz Preserve. The baby was Tecumseh, who a few decades later tried to unite the Native Americans of all tribes in a fight to the finish with the invading Caucasians. Shooting stars like this—one of the most striking of the century—were described by the Shawnee as "the eye of the panther." The great Shawnee leader's name means, "The Panther Coming Across."

The Shawnee village, equivalent to the capital of the Shawnee tribe, was known as Chalahgawtha (from which Chillicothe is derived). It was the fifth Shawnee village in what is now Ohio to bear that name, and there would be two more as the settlers pushed back the frontier. It stood between the community on US 68 now known as Oldtown and the Little Miami River to the west. Tecumseh is said to have been born near a spring, now located on the grounds of a state fish hatchery not more than 100 yards from the preserve. Likely, Tecumseh caught turtles and frogs in the wetlands on the west side of Oldtown Creek. To many, these are hallowed grounds where the spirit of the Shawnee still abides in the woods.

Like many others in the area, Oldtown Creek appears to have cut through deep glacial moraine to reach the limestone and shale bedrock as it tumbled toward Massie Creek and, eventually, the

Little Miami River. Rain falling on adjacent upland moves downward through the porous moraine until it reaches a layer of relatively impervious bedrock. There, it moves laterally to come out of the side of the hill high enough above the elevation of the creekbed to create a wetland. In the preserve, the water appears to come out of the side of the hill in many places. Around the corner, at the fish hatchery, the volume of water was such that it carved a channel in the upper surface of the impervious bedrock, which then carried the water to one spot on the hillside in sufficient quantity to create a spring—the place where Tecumseh was born.

By 1984, the city of Xenia was rapidly expanding to the north. This 43-acre nature preserve was donated to the Green County Park District by residents, most of it in memory of Sara Lee Arnovitz by her descendants. A plaque near the trailhead reads "Give to life the best that you have and the best will come back to you. It is especially meaningful to give to the community which gave so much to Sara Lee Arnovitz and her family: Samuel and Minnie Engilman, parents; Rose Engilman Brusk Gross, sister; and Florence Engilman Koch."

Access

The preserve lies on the north side of Kinsey Road in Greene County's Xenia Township, approximately .8 mile east of US 68 on the north edge of the city of Xenia. A preserve entrance sign and a memorial monument to Mrs. Arnovitz stand alongside the 12-car parking lot.

Trail

At the east end of the parking lot, 15 railroad tie steps lead toward a platform, the creek, and the wetland boardwalk trail. Like other boardwalks made of treated pine, this one is slippery when wet, so caution is in order.

Start walking by turning left past a platform with benches in each corner. From the platform, a three-board-wide walk leads into the wet meadow area. In the late summer, the meadow is especially beautiful with joe-pye weed, ironweed, spotted jewelweed, black-eyed Susan, biennial guara, two species of cattails, ox-eye, wingstem,

*At Arnovitz Preserve, the A-truss bridge leading back to the trailhead
is visible from a platform on the outbound trail.*

three-lobed coneflower, vervain, field thistle, tick trefoils, mountain
mint, boneset, and many other native wet prairie species. The butterfly species found here reveal the presence of nettles and hackberry,
their larval food, somewhere close by.

Earlier in the summer, when red-winged blackbirds are on the
nest, one of the red and yellow-epauletted black males or a brown
female may hover over your head if they feel you are approaching
too close to a nest. The cheery call of the northern yellow-throat will
greet the visitor in May or June.

On the sunny but cool day when I walked the trail, a garter
snake was sunning itself not too far off the trail, a not uncommon
way for a cold-blooded creature to get a start on the day. Frogs are
the favorite food of garter snakes, so I was not surprised to see it in
this wet meadow. I expect that a warm rainy night or two in April
sets the chorus of singing males into action.

The area beside the trail is mowed for a short distance beyond
the platform, but beyond that, the flowers of summer hang close,
providing an excellent opportunity to take close-up pictures. Several

dragonflies and a damselfly posed nicely for my short telephoto lens one August noon. A side platform allows you to rest and look to the right toward Oldtown Creek.

A rather obscure trail to the left leads uphill to a pedestrian access on Hillcrest Drive, allowing runners an opportunity to get off the street and enter the preserve. Ignore the side trail and continue on the main boardwalk toward the observation deck that is in view just ahead.

After a rest and photo opportunity on the platform, return to the main boardwalk, turning left to continue paralleling the creek as it heads northwest toward its intersection with Massie Creek. The boardwalk is sometimes right at the water level here, so be careful.

Patches of the parasitic plant, dodder, can often be seen near the trail in the early fall. After passing the outflow of a spring, the trail turns to the right and heads toward Oldtown Creek. It passes a patch of the tall, summer-blooming, green-headed coneflower and enters the woods, still on boardwalk. Almost immediately it bridges a small side stream. The woods is typical of western Ohio floodplains. The presence of hackberry betrays the calcareous nature of the bedrock and the gravel content of the moraine.

After crossing Oldtown Creek on a multiple king-post bridge with rock-filled gabions for buttresses and piers, the trail continues on boardwalk, swinging upstream. Notice the man-made stepping-stones in the creekbed upstream from the bridge, an earlier accommodation for crossing the stream.

Exiting the young box-elder woods, the trail passes by another wetland, this one higher above the creek. Past the wetland, the trail finally leaves boardwalk, and the trailside flora changes. In the summer, pale jewelweed joins the spotted species and tall lobelia and wingstem come into bloom with their seemingly attendant group of obscure asters, as the autumn equinox nears.

The trail moves back to the creek for a short ways, then begins winding its way up the hillside on a sometimes sod, sometimes dirt surface. A 20-foot, single-span, king-post bridge carries the trail across a small side stream before it rises to pass through young oak-hickory woods on moraine paralleling the boundary fence. Reaching higher ground, there are several large honey locust trees along the trail, then an open area with old field species present. Just beyond a spreading black walnut tree, where a farm field is visible ahead, the trail makes a left oblique turn to follow the boundary. Passing through more young woods, the trail reaches another smaller king-post bridge that spans a drainage from the farm fields to the left. A glance to the right from the bridge reveals the glacial drift nature of the soil on the high land and the limestone bedrock downslope.

Still moving close to the fence, the trail passes young buckeye trees, then reaches a grove of young black locusts where it makes a hard right turn to travel about 100 feet downslope to Oldtown Creek. There it makes a quick right, followed by a quick left. Five steps lead to the 25-foot bridge at the bottom of the stairs to the parking lot.

Sara Lee Arnovitz Preserve is small, off the beaten path, and with a bare minimum of facilities, but it is one of my favorites for a closeup look at the summer flora of a wet meadow. Actually, the wildflower season begins when skunk cabbage blooms in the wet woods on the east side of the creek in late February, and it lasts until frost in October. In between is a lot to see and enjoy, all the while in the spirit company of "The Panther Coming Across" the sky.

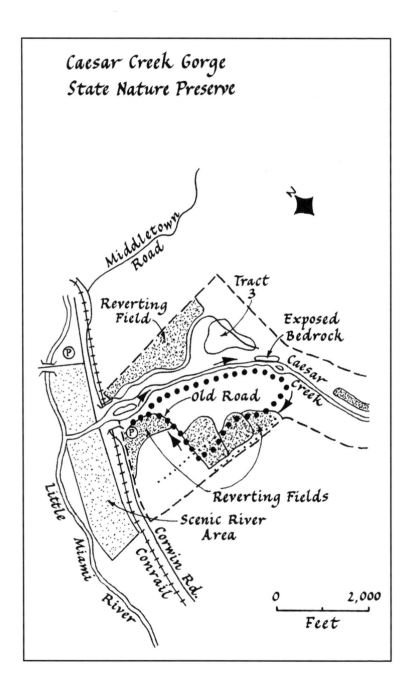

Caesar Creek Gorge
State Nature Preserve

N

Middletown Road

Reverting Field

Tract 3

Exposed Bedrock

Caesar Creek

P

Old Road

P

Reverting Fields

Scenic River Area

Little Miami River

Corwin Rd.

Conrail

0   2,000

Feet

Caesar Creek Gorge
State Nature Preserve

Distance: 2½ miles
Accessibility: Because of the steep terrain,
not wheelchair accessible.
Facilities: Restrooms only. Picnic tables, grills,
swimming beach, boating, campground, additional
restrooms, and bridle trails are available
at nearby Caesar Creek State Park

One hundred eighty-feet-high cliffs of Ordovician lime-stone and shales line the gorge of Caesar Creek where it flows through this 463-acre state nature preserve. Formed by great volumes of glacial meltwater cutting through the bedrock, the gorge provided the outlet for water from the retreating Wisconsinan glacier lying to the northeast.

Though dammed to create Caesar Creek Lake—an Army Corps of Engineers impoundment located just east of the preserve—Caesar Creek supports a rich aquatic animal life, and its banks, a wide variety of plant life. Now heavily wooded with beech, maple, hickory, and oak, even the steep slopes of the valley were probably heavily timbered during the nineteenth century. The uplands show evidence of having at one time been completely cleared for use as pasture and crop fields. Except for a powerline easement, natural succession has been allowed to occur since 1975 when the Department of Natural Resources acquired the land.

Old roadways, foundation stones, fruit trees, and other plant-ing betray the occupancy of the area by settlers. Earlier occupancy by successive cultures of Native Americans is well documented. Many earthworks thought to be of Hopewell origin are found within a few miles of Caesar Creek.

The preserve extends to the east bank of the Little Miami State and National Scenic River area where a river access point is provided. A portion of the Little Miami Scenic Park trail passes through the area close to the parking lot on the former Penn-Central (nineteenth-century Little Miami) Railroad right-of-way.

The spring flora on the sweet soil of the wooded hillsides on both sides of the river is luxuriant. Among the less common species growing on the preserve is shooting star, a plant often associated with prairies but also found in open situations on thin soils above limestone or dolomite cliffs. Although the flowers are pink in color further west, the species is white-flowered here and was, in earlier times, known as "Pride-of-Ohio." On the moist hillsides, the brilliant red firepink blooms at about the same time as the white-blooming, large-flowered trillium fades. The floral show begins in mid-April and lasts into early June. Butterfly-weed, New England aster, and goldenrod are among the flowers in the meadows as summer progresses. Unfortunately, like many natural areas in western Ohio, Caesar Creek preserve has been invaded by bush honeysuckle and garlic mustard, but they detract only a little from the beauty of the place.

Access

Located in Wayne Township in northwestern Warren County, Caesar Creek Gorge State Nature Preserve is located 3 miles north of the village of Oregonia, about 2 miles south of the village of Corwin, on Corwin Road. To reach it from the north, take US 42 to OH 73 at Waynesville, then travel east about .5 mile on OH 73 to the access to Corwin Road. Turn left to travel south on Corwin Road about 2 miles to the preserve parking lot, just beyond a bridge over Caesar Creek on the left side of the road.

Trail

The long-abandoned road that forms the basis of the main trail of the preserve is known as Caesar's Trace. As the story is told, in 1776 a Shawnee party attacked a flatboat on the Ohio River and took captive a black slave called "Cizar." He reportedly was adopted into the tribe and spent much time hunting near a stream he liked so well he named it after himself. When the Kentucky frontiersmen, Simon

High cliffs of Ordovician limestone reach to the water's edge across the stream from the trail at Caesar Creek Gorge State Nature Preserve.

Kenton, who was being held captive at Oldtown further up the Little Miami, was planning his escape, Cizar supposedly advised him to follow "his" creek down to its confluence with the Little Miami to avoid using the well-traveled Indian trail along the west bank of the Little Miami; hence, the name, Caesar's Trace.

About 150 yards up the trace, leave the track, following a narrow foot trail toward the creek. Be aware that there are several wild trails before the real trail is reached, made by fishermen and sightseers. After a drop of 75 feet or so, the trail levels out on a terrace before dropping to a bridge and the floodplain. Escaped garden phlox and green-headed coneflower bloom along here in midsummer. Soon the trail moves closer to the river, where there are side trails to the river's edge made by bank fishermen. After passing through a long bed of scouring rushes, the trail comes out on a gravel bar on the stream. There are nice riffles in the stream here, and there is a spectacular view of the high banks of the gorge.

Traveling through floodplain forest, the trail first leaves the river, then returns to it alongside some rapids. It leaves the river for good as it moves toward the hillside. Here it turns right to move diagonally up the hillside on an old track. As the trail emerges from the woods, it passes through a huge patch of cup plant and alongside basswood, hackberry, buckeye, cedar, and other calciphiles (plants that thrive on a limey substrate). The old fields of the high ground contain a number of prairie plants, such as Canada wild rye, and lots of red cedars. With black locust groves to the right, the trail winds its way near the rim of the gorge. Near the juncture with the old road, it passes a huge black locust. Turn right on the old track and begin the descent toward the parking lot. Shortly after the hillside forest reemerges on the right, the opening for the outgoing trail appears, and the sound of rushing water returns. In a few moments, the parking lot and privies come into view, marking the end of the hike. On the sunny summer day when I last walked this trail, butterflies of many species were my nearly constant companions. It is easy to see why, since many of the plants that sustain butterfly larvae are found along the trail and the flowers that provide the adults with nectar are in the old fields nearby. The diverse habitats of this preserve make it an interesting one to explore at any season.

Cowan Lake
State Park

Distance: 1 mile
Accessibility: A 48-step staircase makes this trail
impassable for the physically challenged.
Facilities: Hiking trails, rental cabins, campground,
picnic areas, swimming beach, boating facilities,
drinking water, and restrooms.

Imagine hundreds of pale yellow lotus blossoms staring up at you from the quiet surface of a lake. You don't even have to get into a boat to get close to these American beauties. At Cowan Lake State Park, on the Lotus Cove Trail, you can look right down into them from a wooden pier that extends out from the shore of the lake.

Immediately following World War II, the state of Ohio began purchasing land along Cowan Creek a few miles south of Wilmington to create a lake for recreational purposes. The dam was completed in 1950, and the 700-acre lake was named for the creek. John Cowan, for whom the creek was named, had been the area's first surveyor.

Cowan Lake State Park was dedicated in June of 1968 with a full complement of modern outdoor recreational facilities. Over the years, park naturalists have developed six fine hiking trails covering about 4½ miles. Some originate from within the campground or at a picnic area. The park office can provide a brochure briefly describing all six. The Lotus Cove Trail is a special treat from July through early September when the American lotus, also referred to as the water lily, blooms.

Access

Cowan Lake State Park is located a little over 5 miles southwest of the city of Wilmington in Vernon and Washington townships of Clinton County. To reach the Lotus Cove Trail parking lot, travel

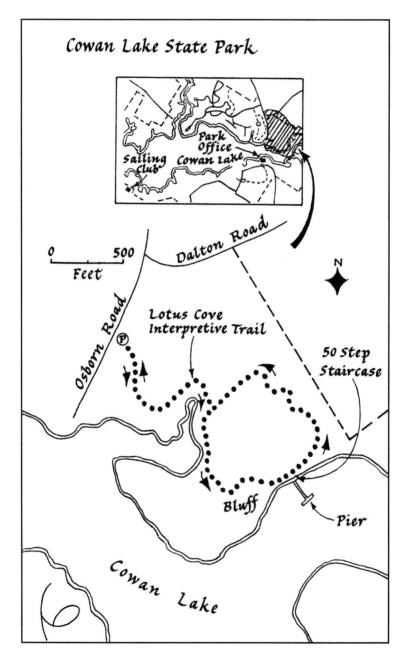

Cowan Lake State Park

Salling Club

Park Office
Cowan Lake

Dalton Road

0   500
Feet

Osborn Road

N

Lotus Cove
Interpretive Trail

50 Step
Staircase

Bluff

Pier

Cowan Lake

OH 730 southwest from Wilmington just over 4 miles to Osborn Road. The parking lot is on the left (north) side of Osborn Road not quite 2 miles after the turn, beyond the campground and cabin area entrance and Dalton Road.

Trail

An interpretive sign at the parking lot briefly describes the trail. Leaving the parking lot, the trail immediately enters what might be described as successional thicket as it moves gently downslope. Groomed via a double pass by bush hog, the trail is bordered here by old field plants, multiflora rose, and small trees such as redbud. Where the forest is older, deciduous trees such as tuliptree overtop dying red cedars that were the early invaders when the field was taken out of farming. There are numbered posts along the trail indicating that there might, at one time, have been a self-guided trail brochure. There was no box dispensing such at the trailhead, though, and none was available at the park office.

Soon swinging to the left through older woods, the trail continues to drop, and the lake becomes visible through the woods to the right. The trail descends to where it is just a few feet above water level in a narrow cove that once was a deep ravine above Cowan Creek. After crossing the duckweed-filled stream at the head of the cove on a wooden bridge, the trail climbs five steps to a terrace.

Paralleling the water's edge, the trail rises gently and, in about 100 feet, arrives at a split in the trail where a sign points the way to Lotus Cove and to the parking lot. Take the right split. The trail passes a pine planting, many large junipers, and lots of regrowth hardwood forest. Climbing to high ground, it arcs right, then begins to parallel the lake shore below. A "wild" trail to the right is worth exploring because it leads to a bluff that overlooks the lotus bed that is the destination of this trail. In midsummer, the sight is absolutely spectacular, with lotuses as far out into the lake as one can see.

Back on the trail, the presence of basswood and chinquapin oak reveals the calcareous substrate. The trail travels around the bluff, with large beech and oak trees on the high ground and cedars on the slope below. When it reaches a post and rail fence, a side trail

Unlike the bullhead lily whose leaves float, the leaves and flowers of the American lotus stand a foot or two above the surface of the water.

descends down 48 steps to the lake and pier. As you approach the lake, you might catch a bullfrog in song and chase the ducks into flight. Most of your attention, however, will be drawn to the immense lotus field. The great, bowl-shaped leaves that stand a foot or two above the water may be two feet across, and the pale yellow flowers, four to eight inches wide. The hundred-foot-long pier that ends in a "T" allows you to take closeup pictures from many angles—beautiful patterns in black and white or color.

At the top of the steps, turn right to continue the loop trail. It soon turns sharply to the left, moving counterclockwise to close the loop. Now traveling through woodland, it crosses a bridge and moves alongside more rail fence before reaching a sign pointing right toward the parking lot.

Even with the slight aggravation of the six-legged hummers that are a constant accompaniment along this lakeshore trail, the hike uncovers a real treasure that every nature lover should behold.

Fort Ancient
State Memorial

Distance: 1 mile
Accessibility: Unpaved surface but relatively level.
Access possible with assistance through most of the trail.
Facilities: Museum, picnic tables, drinking water,
and restrooms.

On a bluff rising 240 feet above the Little Miami River, the prehistoric Hopewell Indians constructed more than 3½ miles of walls varying from 4 to 23 feet in height, using hoes made of animal shoulder blades and hauling earth and limestone slabs by hand. Once thought to have been built for defensive purposes, it was given the name Fort Ancient by early archaeologists.

Evidence now suggests that the site was used as a gathering place for social or religious ceremonies. Archaeologists also believe that the Hopewell Indians (circa 100 B.C. to A.D. 500) were not the only culture to use the site. Strong evidence points to the use of the "south fort" by another group of Indians around A.D. 1200. This culture is referred to as the Fort Ancient culture, named when it was believed that this group had built the "fort."

The preserve was created by a joint resolution of the state legislature in 1891, making it Ohio's first state "park." The 685-acre site is administered as a state memorial by the Ohio Historical Society. Since 1967, the society has operated a small museum on the site designed to develop an understanding among visitors of the highly sophisticated cultures that populated this area long before the coming of white settlers.

Although more than 200 Ohio archaeological sites, including Fort Ancient, are listed on the National Register of Historic Places, fewer than ten have become National Historic Landmarks. Fort

Ancient was so designated in 1964 because of what it had already revealed and what it potentially could reveal about the heritage of prehistoric Indians.

A visit to the museum followed by a walk along the walls of this ancient earthwork stimulates visitors of all ages to imagine the life and times of those more directly tied to the resources of the earth.

Access

Protected for more than 100 years, the site lies on the east side of the Little Miami River in Washington Township of Warren County. It was originally in the Virginia Military District that was settled by Revolutionary War veterans from Virginia. It is located 7 miles southeast of Lebanon on OH 350, reached by turning southeast from I-71 on OH 123. From April through mid-May and after Labor Day through October, the museum and park are open from 10 A.M. to 5 P.M. on Saturdays and 12 to 5 P.M. on Sundays. From Memorial Day weekend through Labor Day, the museum is open from 10 A.M. to 5 P.M. Wednesdays though Saturdays and from 12 to 5 P.M. on Sundays. During that period, the park is open from 10 A.M. to 8 P.M. Wednesdays through Sundays and on holidays. Except for members of the Ohio Historical Society, there may be a charge for admission to the park and/or museum.

Trail

There are three defined areas to Fort Ancient: the large "north fort," the small "middle fort," and the large "south fort." OH 350 cuts across the "north fort" through openings made by the Lebanon to Chillicothe road more than 150 years ago. There may have been openings there when the road was built, but certainly they have been widened since that time. The park entrance is within the "north fort," as is the museum. If the museum is open, spend some time there before you begin your walk. Then walk or drive down the park road to the "south fort," parking at the first available spot after passing through the wall. The trailhead is on the right side of the road, opposite the picnic shelter.

There is an interpretive sign by the parking lot worth reading

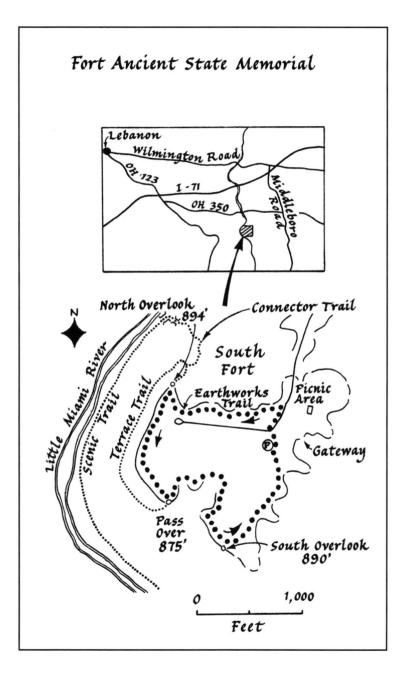

Fort Ancient State Memorial

The view across the valley of the Little Miami River from the overlook at Fort Ancient must be quite similar to that seen by the prehistoric Indians during construction of the famous earthworks.

and similar signs along the trail. At the trailhead, another sign speaks more of this and other trails of the park.

Walking on the grassy trail just inside the wall, travel counterclockwise. After about 1,200 feet, the trail reaches the north overlook area. Take the gravel trail to where you can look northward over the river valley. It is possible to go over the wall here to connect with the terrace trail 69 feet downhill or with the Little Miami Scenic Trail (and Buckeye Trail) on the old Penn-Central Railroad right-of-way 274 feet below. Needless to say, the trail to the old railroad bed is steep.

Returning to the grassy Earthworks Trail, proceed around the perimeter of the "south fort." Note the occasional openings in the wall. Here, the wall and trail are running parallel with the river. The trail drops about 20 feet before reaching a pass over the wall about 1,200 feet south of the north overlook. This is the connection to the other end of the Terrace Trail. No attempt has been made to keep trees from growing on the wall. Protection by the state for more than

100 years has allowed some magnificent specimens to grow on the wall, on the slope below it, and in the fort areas.

The Earthworks Trail now turns left away from the river. After 100 feet, it turns right to drop down into a small valley and cross a creek on a wooden bridge. There are no steps or water bars, so this descent can be slippery. The earth is blanketed with the alien ornamental groundcover myrtle on both sides of the trail at this point. The plant does well in the deep shade of the spreading trees.

Having climbed out of the first valley, the trail drops into a second one where there is a 50-foot bridge and lots more myrtle. A sign tells about the soil of the area and of the early attempts by the Civilian Conservation Corps (CCC) of Great Depression days to retard erosion here. After traveling upslope from the long bridge, the trail again parallels the river alongside the wall.

About 100 yards away is the south overlook. As you approach it, there is a sign telling about wall construction and site occupation by the two Indian cultures. Another tells the story of the Little Miami River. The south overlook is constructed of stone, with a compass rose laid into the floor, probably by CCC workers. At this point, the trail is at 890-foot elevation, 390 feet above the Little Miami River. This point is a great spot to pause for picture taking.

Here, the wall turns north along the top of a ravine. No longer straight, it is less well defined, and the trail does not follow alongside it. To complete your hike, turn north across the area of mowed grass and return to your vehicle.

Though modified by modern man's presence for perhaps two centuries, there remains something sacred about this hike on the paths of the ancients.

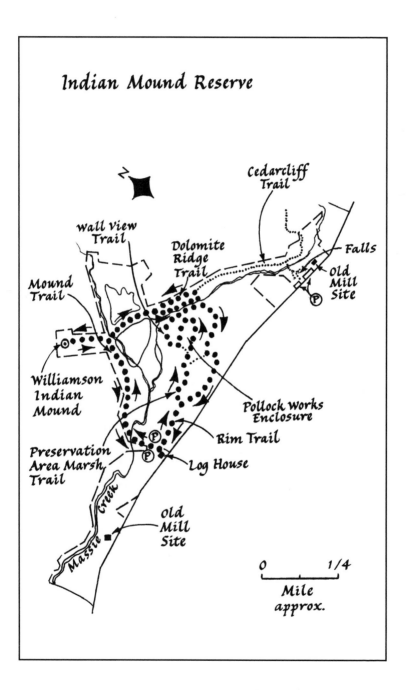

Indian Mound Reserve

Cedarcliff Trail

Wall View Trail

Dolomite Ridge Trail

Falls

Old Mill Site

Mound Trail

Williamson Indian Mound

Pollock Works Enclosure

Rim Trail

Preservation Area Marsh Trail

Log House

Massie Creek

Old Mill Site

0   1/4

Mile approx.

Indian Mound Reserve

Distance: 3 miles
Accessibility: Rugged terrain and trail surface precludes
wheelchair access on most sections of the trail.
Facilities: Restored log cabin, picnic tables, portable
latrines, historic Indian mound and earthworks.

T he gorge near the village of Cedarville through which runs Massie Creek has been a center of activity by humankind for thousands of years. Prehistoric Indians from a number of successive cultures apparently occupied sites close to the gorge, and the area was soon discovered by white settlers as an ideal place to construct water-powered mills.

The formation of the gorge dates back to the last period of glaciation in this area of Ohio. As the ice sheet was melting, torrents of water flowed from it, moving downstream toward the sea. Stream channels were easily made when the water moved through gravel-filled valleys left from earlier periods of glaciation. In other places, however, exposed bedrock blocked the route, so narrow gorges were cut in the rock by the sand, sediment, and gravel-laden meltwater. Such was the case at Cedarville, where a massive formation of Silurian-age dolomite lies just beneath the surface of the land. To the east, the hard rock dips below strata that is more easily eroded. To the west, it is gone, probably removed by earlier continental glaciation.

Glacial meltwater cut through the same dolomite at Clifton when the Little Miami River was establishing its channel, at Spring-field when the route of the Mad River was shaping up, and at many other places in east central Ohio.

The Cedarville formation was described as a separate strati-graphic unit by state geologist Edward Orton in 1871. Doubtless the village name was derived from the presence of red cedars growing in the shallow soil over the dolomite.

The Greene County Park District has brought together under one management areas originally belonging to a number of individuals and other agencies. The 165-acre Indian Mound Reserve straddles the Massie Creek gorge, beginning near the western edge of the village of Cedarville. The park includes the large conical Williamson Mound, thought to be of Adena origin, the Pollock Works, a hilltop "fortification" believed of Hopewell origin, at least two mill sites, and the ruins of an early industry settling pond. Together, they offer a journey through a large span of history in a nice natural setting.

Access

Located in Cedarville Township of Greene County, this reserve lies on the north side of OH 42 less that 1 mile west of its intersection with OH 72 in downtown Cedarville. It is open without charge during daylight hours throughout the year.

Trails

Stop at the entrance closest to town for a look at the stone arch dam, referred to as Cedar Cliff Falls, that was built in 1887 to drive a turbine power plant alongside the Harbison flour mill. The mill was constructed in 1868 and operated until about 1917. It stood on the near side of the dam. A wide-angle lens will capture a splendid portrait of the "falls" from the footbridge.

At the next entrance to the west, park and then study the relocated log house standing close by. Contemplate what it would be like to be part of a large extended family living summer and winter in such a house.

The trail leaves the right edge of the parking lot, headed up a mowed trail between fields. Pale and spotted jewelweed grow side by side here in midsummer. A couple hundred yards after passing through an overgrown osage orange fence line into the woods, the trail divides. The mowed trail to the right looks like it could be an old highway route. Take the trail to the left, labeled "to enclosure," and head downslope past young trees and thicket. You will enter a wetland covering several acres, with lots of wildflowers and butterflies in midsummer.

The falls at Indian Mound Reserve are created by a man-made structure left from an era when water drove American industry.

After reentering woods, the trail crosses a small footbridge and soon arrives at another split, "the enclosure" again pointed out as being to the left. Following the left trail leads to a climb and to arrival at an opening in the Pollock Works wall. Turn right after passing into the enclosure, heading toward a plateau between the present-day Massie Creek channel on the far left and an older channel over the cliff to the right. No wonder the builders of this earthworks chose this spot, surrounded as it is by valley. The area looks like it may have once been pasture, but it is now covered with small trees and lots of club moss, usually an acid soil indicator (we appear to be above the influence of the dolomite).

Circumnavigate the mesa area, then turn right at the first side trail downslope (the Wall View Trail). The route leads around the side of the hill where Wright State University students have recently been conducting some archaeological explorations. Pass up the opportunity to take wild side trails over to the creek and, instead, follow the trail along the talus below the cliff face. Eventually you reach creek level. Here, the opposite wall of the gorge is visible.

At this point, if you are tired of hiking or if the water is too high or too cold to wade, take the trail to the right. It circles clockwise up the old stream channel to cross a bridge and turn left. It then arcs to the right beneath the cliff alongside OH 42. Notice the large glacial erratics on the talus slope, probably cleared from a field or roadbed above and rolled over the cliff. The old road on which the trail travels leads back to the parking lot.

It is possible to wade across the stream to explore the other side of the creek and visit Williamson Mound. The alternative is to return to the parking lot and then walk there on what looks like a road and vehicle bridge that originates on the west side of the log house. The vehicle access to the mound is only for private residences on the far side of the creek.

After crossing the bridge on the route from the log house, the trail turns to gravel. A short distance beyond, a trail that enters the woods to the right leads upstream on an old road. Ahead to the right on the floodplain is the site of the "middle reservoir." This 20-acre pond served as a settling basin for toxic effluent that arrived there through an elaborate system of pipes, sluiceways, and ditches from the Hager Board and Paper Co. mill that operated upstream until the late 1930s.

Just beyond a bench by the trail, a post announces Cedar Trail to the right and Mound Trail to the left. The Mound Trail goes uphill on a rocky trail through an opening in the cliff. From there, it climbs across a mowed field to the base of the Williamson Mound. A sign tells the story of the mound and how it came to be preserved.

Returning to the creek valley, turn left on the Cedar Trail. It follows the levee of the old middle reservoir until it drops down close to creek level. The trail moves right up against the cliff and, before long, comes to the foot trail ford. Beyond that point, at a break in the cliff face, it climbs steeply on rocks and railroad ties to meet a trail that goes both left and right. There is no sign. The Cedarcliff Trail to the right leads upstream to connect to the parking lot at Cedar Cliff Falls. The Dolomite Ridge Trail, which you can take to the left, heads downstream. Dolomite "Ridge" is a misnomer; more correctly, it should be a "cliff top" or "rim" trail. The property fence, with its attendant rolls of old fence and piles of farm trash, lies just to the right of the trail, and the Cedarville dolomite cliff is to the left. The trail eventually descends to join the trail that leads back to the parking lot.

The hepatica is especially beautiful in early spring on the trail between the Pollock Works and the creek. The wildflowers and butterflies of summer near the marsh are superb, and, of course, the best way to see industrial and Indian archaeological sites is after the leaves drop, perhaps even with a light sprinkling of snow to emphasize the straight lines of human-made structures.

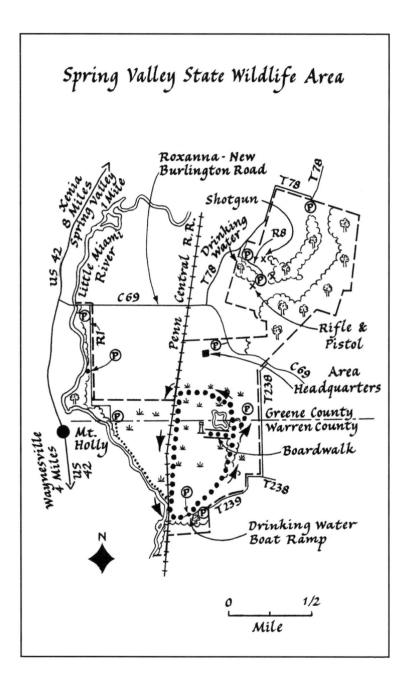

Spring Valley State Wildlife Area

Roxanna - New
Burlington Road

Xenia 8 Miles
Spring Valley 1 Mile
US 42

Little Miami River

Shotgun

T78

Drinking water T78

R8

Penn Central R.R.

C 69

R1

Rifle & Pistol

Area Headquarters

C 69

T238

Waynesville 4 Miles
US 42

Mt. Holly

Greene County
Warren County

Boardwalk

T238

Drinking Water
Boat Ramp

T139

N

0   1/2
Mile

Spring Valley
State Wildlife Area

Distance: 2 miles
Accessibility: Trail along west side of marsh
accessible with assistance.
Facilities: Drinking water, public hunting and fishing,
shooting ranges, archery course, and
boat launching ramp.

Before it was a state wildlife area, part of this land was the Sinclair Fur Farm. After the state acquired the first parcel of land in 1953, it began making improvements by expanding the lake to its present 80 acres. There is public fishing from bank and boat, but the area is perhaps best known for the large number of unusual birds that can be seen there all year long. A boardwalk, constructed using funds from the "Do Something Wild" tax-checkoff program, provides safe access to the 150-acre lake and marsh, so plan to carry binoculars and/or a spotting scope.

One late summer evening as I walked the trail along the north edge of the lake, I watched two young red foxes come onto the trail 100 feet ahead of me box and parry in a frenzy of juvenile fun. On a warm day in April, noise of calling frogs was so loud that I could hardly carry on a conversation with my hiking companion.

The plants that bloom here range from skunk cabbage in February to witch hazel in November. Massasaugua rattlesnakes have been spotted in years past, but it is highly unlikely a hiker would ever encounter one of these timid creatures. The Buckeye Trail passes along the western edge of the 842-acre area, and the old Penn-Central (nineteenth-century Little Miami) Railroad right-of-way is a part of the Little Miami Scenic Park open for hiking and bicycling. A parking lot and a boat launching ramp provide easy access to the Little Miami Scenic River that flows along the western boundary of the Wildlife Area.

Access

Originally in the Virginia Military District of the Northwest Territory established in 1784 to satisfy the claims of Virginia's soldiers who fought during the Revolution, the area now is a part of two Ohio counties: Spring Valley Township of Greene County and Wayne Township of Warren County. Located 8 miles south of Xenia off US 42, the area entrance is on Roxanna-New Burlington Road.

Traveling east from US 42 on Roxanna-New Burlington Road, ignore the signs on the right that identify the wildlife area headquarters, going on to Township Road 238, a total distance of about 1.5 miles. Less than .5 mile south (right) on this road, there is a drive on the right that leads to a parking lot. Park there.

Trail

The trail exits the lot through the wooded fencerow on the left and angles immediately to the west toward the lake and marshes. Remember that where there are furred, finned, and feathered wetland creatures, there are six-legged chitinous creatures of all shapes and sizes on which they feed, some of which feed on humans. During the warm months, consider protective clothing and/or repellents.

The trail winds its way downhill through successional woodland, first passing a trail to the left, then, when it reaches the bottom of the hill, to the right. Ignore them and continue ahead, following a gravel trail to the ramp that leads up to the boardwalk. Tread stealthily on the boardwalk so you do not scare off any wildlife close by. Be sure to watch for American bittern among the cattails, looking for all the world like one of them. I have often photographed ducks, geese, turtles, dragonflies, and frogs at close range along this boardwalk. Climb the tower and scan the area through your binoculars. Be sure to watch the sky, where you may be lucky enough to spot an osprey looking for a meal.

Trace your steps back to solid ground. Head back toward the parking lot and take the trail to the left through the woods. Follow it north, then west, passing alternately by young woods, bushy thicket, and emergent aquatic vegetation. In the spring, male common yellow-throats stake out their territories with a "witchity, witchity,

*Canada geese can be seen year-round along the trail
at Spring Valley State Wildlife Area.*

witchity, witch." In the summer, mockingbirds, brown thrashers, and other fruit-eating birds enjoy the fruit of the ubiquitous multiflora rose. Listen for one of three species of rail that might be found here. Consult a good bird identification guide for the ranges and unusual calls of these secretive marsh birds.

After .5 mile, the trail turns south for a long stretch along the west bank of the lake. Butterflies enjoy the flowers of summer here, and as you get further south, the open water of the lake comes into view. Look for dabbling ducks, geese, coots, moorhens, and grebes. Just to the right in a wooded corridor is the state's major rails-to-trails project—the Little Miami Scenic Trail. With the help of the Greene and Clark county park districts, the trail will one day be completed from Springfield to the east suburbs of Cincinnati, with much of it paved for bicycle travel. It is also the route of the Buckeye Trail, and soon will be the official route of the North Country Trail through this part of Ohio.

At the corner of the lake, turn left along the shoreline and cross the parking lot to pick up the trail again. It passes through marsh and thicket, and, as it moves onto higher ground, young woods, before meeting up with the entrance trail. I usually turn left to revisit the boardwalk before heading home. A right turn will take you back to your vehicle.

Spring Valley State Wildlife Area is full of things that creep, cry, crawl, call, hop, run, fly, and burst into bloom. You will want to walk its trail often to sharpen your knowledge of all things natural.

Sugarcreek Reserve

Distance: 2½ miles
Accessibility: Access by physically challenged would
be difficult, but not impossible given a strong assistant.
Facilities: Picnic tables, restrooms, archery center, drinking water,
riding center and bridle trails, planted prairie,
and group campsites (permits required).

O hio has many streams with the name Sugar Creek. The two branches of this Sugar Creek drain the extreme southeast corner of Montgomery County, then cross into Greene County to empty into the Little Miami River just south of Bellbrook. Though situated astride the south branch of Sugar Creek in Greene County's Sugar Creek Township, 596-acre Sugarcreek Reserve is a facility of the Park District of Dayton-Montgomery County. Much of it was once farmland, but today, thanks to natural processes and park district land management techniques, it offers a variety of natural habitats. This variety makes it a fine place to hike, and the park district has developed five miles of hiking trails for visitors to enjoy.

Access

To get to Sugarcreek Reserve from the interstate system, travel I-675 south from I-70 or north from I-75 to OH 725. Travel east on OH 725. Immediately after crossing from Montgomery County into Greene County, turn right (south) on Wilmington-Dayton Road. After curving left, then right, then left (about 1.5 miles), Wilmington-Dayton Road makes a sharp right turn to the south. At this point Conference Road originates straight ahead, heading due east. The park entrance is .5 mile east of this intersection on the north (left) side of Conference Road. It is open without charge from 8 A.M. until dusk except Christmas and New Year's Day.

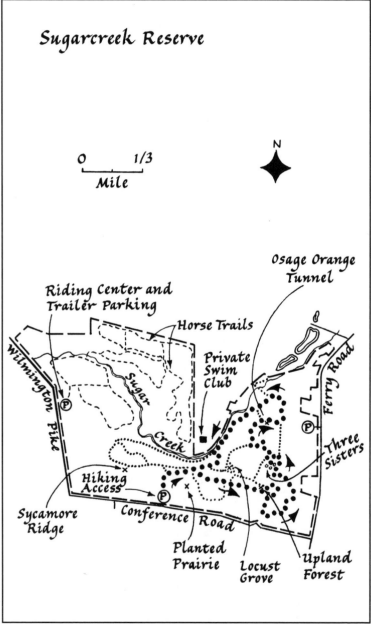

Sugarcreek Reserve

Trails

At the far side of the parking lot, an arrow on a sign points straight ahead to "hiking trail." To the left and right are former agricultural fields undergoing secondary succession. Young trees are beginning to invade the one on the left but are being kept out of the one on the right by controlled burning.

After passing through an archway of young maple trees, the trail reaches a "T". Turn right, visit the information kiosk, then continue heading east toward another bulletin board where maps, including one that shows the mileage of various numbered sections of the trail, and self-guided trail brochures are available. There are numbered posts throughout the reserve to help you determine exactly where you are hiking.

Start hiking on trail #3. The "Three Sisters" self-guided trail uses this trail for much of its path. Where it does, posts with letters corresponding to the letters in the "Three Sisters Trail Guide" appear alongside the trail. At stop "A," the brochure tells about how the land was cleared and farmed and about how it is now being maintained as a fire-managed meadow. An interpretive sign explains the park district's forward-thinking land stewardship program. A prairie plant brochure invites you to test your skills at identifying some of the native grasses and forbs. Stay on trail #3 as it loops right into the prairie. Here, too, trail #4 joins from the left, then quickly exits to the left heading toward the creek.

Continuing on trail #3 takes you past some young trees, then past more prairie. There is a small pond off to the left and a powerline overhead. Does the kestrel box on the pole look like it's being used? At stop "B," a sign tells of buffalo, bluestem, and much more. Unlike at "A" where the meadow contained mostly plants of Eurasian origin, including the grasses, at "B" the plants are grasses and forbs native to the original prairies of western Ohio. You may have noticed the young burr oak on the edge of the prairie. This fire-resistant species occurs in "oak openings" of the wet prairies of west central Ohio and belongs with the herbaceous species. What is special here is the great prairie that the park has been able to establish.

Trail #3 continues ahead, passing the entrance to #6 on the left. Now entering a young woods, it passes station "C"—a wild black cherry stand—then curves to the left passing a group campsite. Beyond a large honey locust tree, there is another trail juncture and station "D," where the trail guide talks about water, ravines, and woodlands. After losing trail #6 and the "Three Sisters Trail" to the left, this hike, still on trail #3, descends a steep hill to a creekbed. Beneath chinquapin oak, basswood, redbud, and hackberry, large slabs of limestone seem appropriate for use as steps. Crossing the small tributary on stepping-stones, the trail climbs to a small shelter where a park map shows your location.

Now with a gravel surface, the trail travels alongside the stream. Note the large glacial erratics lying on top of the great slabs of limestone bedrock in the creek. Every now and then among the six- to eight-inch trees stands a much older tree with wide-spreading branches—a "wolf tree"—that probably grew here when the area was still being grazed. Making a counterclockwise loop, the trail rises gently to higher land where there are some nice open-grown beech, maple, walnut, and tuliptree trees. How these missed the sawyer, I am not sure.

Soon the trail winds its way back downhill to the creek on what looks like an old roadway. After following alongside the creek for a ways, it crosses on some more giant limestone slabs. Note the signs on the right warning that the land is an archery area and closed to hikers.

Next the trail reaches a junction where trail #3 goes straight ahead and our hike heads left, going uphill to the location of the famous old white oaks known as the "Three Sisters." An interpretive sign and post "F" in the printed trail guide both do a good job of telling the story of these massive trees that were growing on this hillside when Columbus was but a lad. Being in the presence of something living that was nearly ten times my age was, somehow, very humbling.

You can opt to return to the stream bottom and follow the right loop of trail #3 or continue following this trail on beyond the awesome oaks. Given the latter choice, note that at an intersection

The osage orange "tunnel" is a reminder of an earlier time when the tree species was used as a living fence around many pastures in the Midwest.

ahead, lettering on a stone slab indicates that this was once Conference Road, the road that presently travels along the park's southern boundary. Turn right on #3/6, part of the Three Sisters self-guided hike.

Passing through young woods, the trail rises slightly, then dips to go by a grove of osage oranges. The trail turns left where post "G" prompts you to read about osage oranges in the trail guide. At a "T" with trail #5, head right toward the "Osage Orange Tunnel." Now wide and grassy, the trail goes through abandoned field that has now reached the "thicket" stage of succession. At another "T," turn right toward an incredible old osage orange fencerow planted more than a hundred years ago. Granite boulders, cleared from the adjoining field to make it tillable, are piled against the trees. A kiosk with a map identifies your location. Up the "tunnel" to the right under the "hedgeapple" tree sits an old iron bench, a place to pause and contemplate how far and how fast our agrarian civilization has come. Picture in your mind the hard work required to clear the field with oxen and "stone boat." It would also take great faith in the forces of nature to believe that plant cuttings will grow into a fence.

Beyond the "tunnel," turn left at the "T" with alternate trail #3. It curves around the hillside, passing a trail to the left not on the map. You soon arrive at a map kiosk and the intersection with trail #2. Now just about as far from the parking lot as you can get without crossing Sugar Creek, turn left to "head for the barn."

After being joined by two trails coming in from the left, trail #2 drops into the creek valley to follow it upstream. It travels along the creek for nearly .5 mile, passing once again under the powerline. In the summer, there are beautiful butterflies and wildflowers under the powerline, and when the creek is not too dry, you can hear water passing over riffles.

Just after crossing over a small side stream on a wooden bridge with handrails, take trail #4 to the left, climbing ten steps to start an ascent over layers of bedrock toward the central area of the park. Rest on the rock wall at the top and proceed on the grassy trail past invading prairie plants. In late August, goldfinches dash in and out of here to feed on the tall coreopsis seeds.

Trail #5 joins from the left as you continue heading west on #4. The "H" post alongside the trail indicates you are again on the Three Sisters hike. This station, the last, tells about the esker beneath your feet.

Trails #4 and #3 intersect before reaching the kiosk area; backtrack from here on #3. The hike ends with the short walk between the meadows back to the parking lot.

The Narrows Reserve

Distance: 2½ miles
Accessibility: Terrain and trail surface preclude
access by physically challenged.
Facilities: Interpretive center, drinking fountain, restrooms,
and canoe launch at trailhead only.
Occasional benches along trail.

Nearly 12,000 years ago, when the Wisconsinan glacier was melting off the land we now call Ohio, meltwater flowing south sought outlets to the sea. In many places, the meltwater was blocked by the ice from using preglacial river valleys, so temporary lakes developed in front of the glacier until the water rose high enough to find a cull where it could cut a new channel and continue its downhill flow.

Such was the case in the southwestern corner of Greene County, where water broke over a cull and cut a new channel for what we now call the Little Miami River. This steep-sided and narrow section of the Little Miami River valley is referred to as "The Narrows."

In the early seventies, the Little Miami River—from its confluence with the Ohio to near its headwaters—was designated first a state and later a national scenic river. To protect the geologically significant narrows of the river, the Department of Natural Resources acquired 162 acres of land on the west side of the river south of Indian Ripple Road. It was subsequently leased to the Greene County Park District and opened to the public as The Narrows Reserve.

There are now close to three and a half miles of trails traversing this reserve. The upper and lower ends of the reserve carry trails on the upland areas, and in the middle section a single trail parallels the river. A free-flowing, unimpounded river, the Little Miami periodically overflows its channel and covers its natural floodplain. Through the narrows, where there is little floodplain, the river runs high and fast during storm events, and the River Trail becomes inundated and, of course, impassable.

Access

Located in Beaver Creek Township of Greene County, The Narrows Reserve is easily reached by traveling west from Xenia on US 35 to Factory Road. Turn left (south) and go 1.4 miles to Indian Ripple Road, where the entrance to the reserve is directly ahead. The park is open every day until sunset.

Trail

Hit the River Trail from the parking lot by using the gravel canoe launch access road. The trail stays away from the river most of the time, but now and again moves to the riverbank. Tall sycamores are joined by hackberry, ash, boxelder, and other floodplain species to make a wooded corridor clear through the reserve. The sound of rushing water and/or happy canoeists will be evident to your left from time to time. After walking about ⅙ mile and crossing a small footbridge, you will see a trail coming in from the right. This is our return route, the Vista Trail, that goes north toward the interpretive center and parking lot. For now, stay on the River Trail, where there are a couple of huge sycamores just beyond this trail juncture.

For the next 1,400 feet, the River Trail is the only footpath through the narrows. Small footbridges span streams entering the river, and sometimes the trail "bellies out" in low areas that never seem to dry out. When the floodplain all but disappears, the forest along the trail changes to the oaks and hickories of Ohio hillsides. The floodplain soon reappears, and the trail momentarily leaves the river as it passes a juncture with the Cold Springs Trail, from which you will later reenter the River Trail.

Head straight down a long corridor through trees, eventually moving very close to the bank. After crossing a side stream, it is necessary to walk up the creek a short ways to where you take the Big Wood Trail to the left. Back away from the stream is a camping

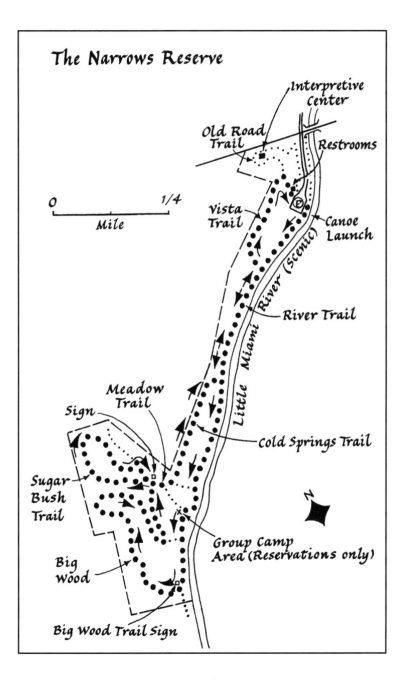

The Narrows Reserve

Interpretive Center

Old Road Trail

Restrooms

Vista Trail

Canoe Launch

Little Miami River (Scenic)

River Trail

0   1/4
Mile

Meadow Trail

Sign

Cold Springs Trail

Sugar Bush Trail

Big Wood

Group Camp Area (Reservations only)

Big Wood Trail Sign

*Among the many young trees growing on the floodplain of the
Little Miami River stand a few giant sycamores.*

area available to canoeing and hiking groups on a reservation basis
only. It's easy to see where the Big Wood Trail gets its name, for it
passes under oak trees perhaps two and a half centuries old.

Here the trail is mowed grass along the left side of an open
field. At the end of the meadow, the trail splits one more time, with
a trail that you ignore going to the right and the Big Wood Trail,
now narrow, heading back toward the river. Soon a sign indicates
that the Big Wood Trail turns to the right. Though an unmapped
trail continues downstream, go right, heading west across floodplain
and then uphill toward higher ground. Near a large thorny honey-
locust, the trail turns toward the north through oak-maple forest. A
mixture of young and older open-grown trees, this area must have
at one time been pastured.

The trail now swings uphill on gravelly moraine on what looks
like an old sugarbush road, soon reaching a gate and old fence
perhaps 100 feet from the west boundary fence. There it turns in a

clockwise direction through more tall timber as it drops down to cross an unbridged gully. You rise once more before beginning a descent alongside a gully, headed toward the meadow where the campground is located. At the corner of the field, a sign identifies the trail being exited as the Big Wood Trail. A mowed trail straight ahead connects with the River Trail across the meadow. Take a sharp left turn along the uphill edge of the meadow, which leads to another intersection.

If you want to add the Sugar Bush Trail to your walk, head left, up and across a dry run where a sign will identify its entrance. It adds another ¼ mile to your walk, carrying you to an oak-maple forest on the upland and then back to this point. Traveling to the right about 100 feet from the Meadow Trail sign will bring you to the entrance of the Cold Springs Trail. Turn left to follow this trail back to the River Trail.

This woodland trail presents a challenge by way of a creek crossing almost immediately. Try going upstream 50 feet or so to cross on flat rocks. At a trail juncture, stay left and follow what looks like an old road that parallels the boundary fence. Fifteen or twenty feet of boardwalk helps you keep your feet dry in the area of the cold springs. A huge cedar tree stands like a sentinel alongside the trail. Nearly level spots look like they could have once been home and garden sites. From there, a long straight trail carries the hiker back to the floodplain and a connector to the River Trail.

After traveling 1,250 feet upstream, take the Vista Trail off to the left. Following it takes the hiker across a T-shaped bridge, up a creek and down to another creekbed, then up a rocky trail to the vista. From a bench, you can see the trees at the same elevation on the far side of the valley. The trail is now close enough to Indian Ripple Road that the sound of traffic is again audible. The trail now descends to a bridge, then comes back up to a fence lined with open-grown trees. After crossing several more bridged gullies, the trail reaches the track of an old road. A sign indicates that the trail to the left is closed. Turning right, the trail begins its descent over flat rocks and railroad tie water bars eventually to reach an opening in the split rail fence by the trailhead parking lot.

Except for an occasional runner, you will likely have most of this trail to yourself. The sound of rushing water brings solace to many. It is excellent habitat for barred owls, and I exchanged hoots with several during my downstream journey through the floodplain forest. Try it. You might be surprised when one answers your best "who cooks for you, who cooks for you all."

Mill Creek
Watershed

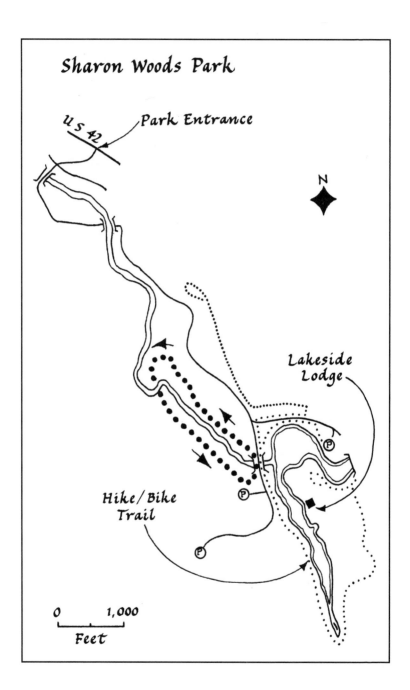

Sharon Woods Park

US 42

Park Entrance

N

Lakeside
Lodge

Hike/Bike
Trail

0   1,000
Feet

25

Sharon Woods Park

Distance: 1¼ miles
Accessibility: Only parts of this loop trail are
negotiable by wheelchair with assistance.
Facilities: Picnic tables and shelters, restrooms, boating,
golf course, historical village, bicycle trail, visitor center,
Parcours fitness trail, drinking water, ballfields,
and dedicated nature preserve.

Sharon Woods is a 737-acre regional park owned and operated by the Hamilton County Park District in the greater Cincinnati area. It was the first park opened by the district, with initial purchase and construction of the first facilities taking place in 1932. Early development was made possible with help from the depression-era Civilian Conservation Corps and Works Progress Administration. In 1937, 34-acre Kreis Lake (named for one of the first park commissioners) brought an added recreational dimension to the park. Many additional facilities have since been added, making it a true multiuser recreation area for southwestern Ohio's million-plus population.

Sharon Woods is a land parcel of impressive natural diversity. Central to the park is Sharon Creek, with its small waterfalls and exposed bedrock. The surrounding slopes possess deciduous forest in various stages of maturity, with some areas sporting magnificent oak, hickory, beech, maple, tuliptree, and black walnut trees.

The topography of the area is rugged, with Ordovician-aged limestones and shales exposed in deep-cut gorges and ravines. Evidence of the earlier existence of shallow, warm saltwater oceans is attested to by the brachiopods, bryozoans, and crinoid fossils found in the bedrock. The Sharon Woods area was last covered by ice about 20,000 years ago during the furthest advance of the Wisconsinan Glacier. The presence of an occasional glacial erratic—a large or small stone of igneous origin, transported to the area from its place

The geology of the area is well interpreted by displays along the Richard H. Durrell Gorge Trail in Sharon Woods Park.

of origin by the advancing ice sheets—provides witness to the coming and going of glaciers.

Considering how close the park is to heavily populated areas, the wildlife of the area is quite diverse. The park district manages for wildlife diversity by keeping some open land and designing trails to provide some unfragmented forest; nevertheless, most of the species found here are those that have accommodated to coexisting with humankind.

In 1977, a 20.86-acre tract along Sharon Creek below Kreis dam was set aside as a state scenic nature preserve, and a trail through the preserve was named for Professor Richard H. Durrell, a former park commissioner and Ohio Natural Areas Council member and a moving force in natural area protection in Ohio. Professor Durrell, now retired from the University of Cincinnati Geology Department, made geology come alive for hundreds of students through his slide shows and field trips. The trail is of moderate difficulty. A detailed educational folder about this trail can be picked up at the park visitor center or be obtained by mail from the district office by calling (513) 521-PARK. It is this trail that is described here.

Entry to Sharon Woods, like to all facilities of the Hamilton County Park District, requires possession of an annual permit, which costs $3.00, or payment of a $1.00 daily entry fee.

Access

Sharon Woods is located just east of US 42, south from I-275, in the northeastern part of Hamilton County. There is an entrance to the park on the east side of US 42 (Lebanon Road), approximately 1 mile south of the I-275 interchange. It can also be reached through an entrance on the south side of Kemper Road .7 mile east of the Kemper/Lebanon Road (US 42) intersection.

The parking area for the Richard H. Durrell Gorge Trail is on the south side of the park road that leads to the golf course. It is at the east end of the bridge over Sharon Creek.

Trail

After parking, walk the tarmac path back across the Kreis dam/bridge to the trailhead. Here you will find a set of steps that lead to below the dam. Note the half-century-old structure of precisely fitted stonework created by workers of the Works Progress Administration (WPA) in 1937; it was built with a craftsmanship hard to find or too expensive to afford nowadays.

The pond below the dam serves as a catch point for fish coming over the dam during high water. It also harbors creatures such as turtles, water snakes, frogs, and aquatic insects. Sometimes in the summer, when not much water is coming over the dam, it gets covered with an emerald green coating of the small floating plant, duckweed.

Return to the trailhead to start the Gorge Trail hike. After reading the entry sign material, head down the railroad tie steps to the graveled trail. (The day I walked the trail, I could not find any numbered posts to correlate with the printed trail guide I was carrying, but perhaps they have now been replaced.) The trail drops to about 20 feet above stream level. Shortly, a sign reminds walkers of good trail etiquette. There are two small but pretty falls in the creek below, each slowly changing as natural forces cause the rims of the falls to erode. The trail rises ever so gently up the hillside away from the creek. Occasional handrails assure hikers of safety next to steep slopes. Years of erosion on the hillside to the right have exposed many tree roots.

In the past this gorge was considered a good place to collect Ordovician fossils, but with the coming of the dam and subsequent reduction in undercutting and stream tumbling of rock rubble, few new ones are being exposed. For their own safety and for the preservation of the natural integrity of the area, visitors are required to remain on the trails.

A hundred yards or so down the valley, a directional sign turns hikers up a set of steps to the right away from the creek. A sign at the top of the steps challenges the hiker to think about the kinds of trees nearby. Large oaks and hickories are slowly being replaced by shade-tolerant sugar maples. The understory consists of pawpaws and alien shrubs and vines whose seeds have been carried here in the droppings of birds from nearby residential areas.

The trail turns to the left, downstream, still climbing uphill and apparently using an old road bed. Along the trail lies a granite glacial erratic, proof that the last glacier did reach this area. At the top of the hill there is a triangular patch of the nonnative climbing euonymus where a side trail to the right leads to a nearby picnic area. Take the trail to the left to travel on downstream, slightly away from the rim of the gorge. The gorge is close to 100 feet deep here, so you look out over the tops of tall trees on the left. After a bit of twisting and turning on the high ground and after passing a service access to your right, the trail descends into the gorge via a set of steps and a sloped gravel path. At one time, the trail came directly down the hillside, resulting in considerable erosion. Where the trail turns to become a wide boulevard that heads upstream toward a bridge, a free-standing interpretive display tells of the fossils of the Ordovician limestones and shales. It is worth a complete reading.

The trail passes the remains of a mill race that a century ago carried water to a mill once located in the area. The high cliff downstream, known as the 90-foot Lookout, sports spectacular icicles in the wintertime. Please heed the fences and don't leave the trail to explore, even on what look like side trails. Enjoy and photograph it from here.

Now heading upstream, the trail soon reaches a bridge across Sharon Creek where another interpretive sign tells of the nature of this ancient streambed. Tall fences along the trail remind visitors to stay out of the creekbed.

The trail is lined with large bush honeysuckles that need to be removed to allow native shrubs to grow. The sound of running water to the left suggests the presence of a small waterfall and, unfortunately, a "wild" side trail leads there. From here, the broad, crushed limestone trail gently climbs to a summit, where another interpretive sign tells about the geologic history of the area and points out the presence of glacial erratics that arrived here perhaps 29,000 years ago. The sign correctly suggests that a good way to learn more about Ice Age Hamilton County is to visit the Cincinnati Museum of Natural History at the Union Terminal Historical Center. The trail now arcs gently to the left as it descends to the road at the parking lot side of the dam/bridge.

Though the landscape along the 1¼-mile trail has suffered badly at the hand of man, the geologic story that is unfolded in the valley is well worth witnessing.

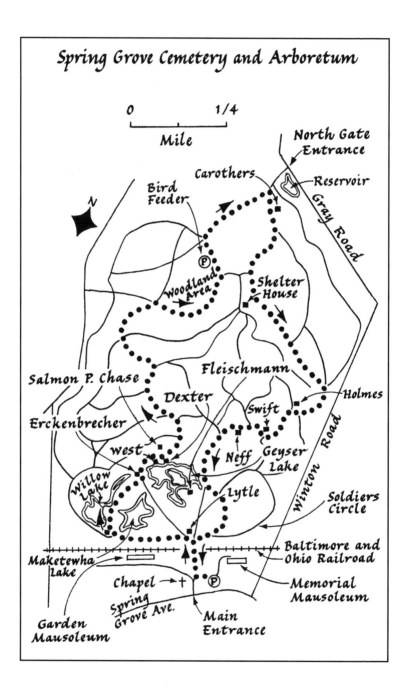

Spring Grove Cemetery and Arboretum

0   1/4
Mile

North Gate Entrance

Carothers

Reservoir

Gray Road

Bird Feeder

N

Woodland Area

Shelter House

Salmon P. Chase

Fleischmann

Dexter

Swift

Holmes

Erckenbrecher

West

Neff

Geyser Lake

Willow Lake

Lytle

Winton Road

Soldiers Circle

Maketewha Lake

Baltimore and Ohio Railroad

Chapel

Spring Grove Ave.

Main Entrance

Memorial Mausoleum

Garden Mausoleum

Spring Grove Cemetery and Arboretum

Distance: 1½ miles
Accessibility: Totally accessible, with alternate
route to avoid steep hill.
Facilities: Blacktopped roads. Restrooms at office.

Cincinnati's Spring Grove Cemetery and Arboretum covers 733 acres of forested hillside and includes 14 lakes, 35 miles of paved roads, and over 170,000 interments. It was established in 1845 during the heyday of what historians refer to as the "rural cemetery movement." Like its counterparts in most other major eastern cities, it was planned as a place for permanent burial sites in a beautiful natural setting close enough to where people lived and worked to be relatively easy to reach, both for funeral services and as a parklike area where citizens could escape the hustle and bustle of the city.

The cemetery was originally laid out by Cincinnati architect Howard Daniels, but the landscape style and grace for which it is famous was imparted to the grounds by the midnineteenth-century, Prussian-born landscape architect, Adolph Strauch. He served as Spring Grove's superintendent for 27 years and added his touch to many local parks and estates as well as to other cemeteries around the country.

Built in the horse-and-buggy era, the cemetery was served by a "turnpike" built by the cemetery corporation in 1845 that connected with roads that led to the city. Five years later, when the Cincinnati, Hamilton, and Dayton Railroad (to become the Baltimore and Ohio in this century) pushed north to connect those cities, an attractive stone overpass was constructed that did not detract from the design of the grounds.

The striking Norman Gothic gatehouse that lies on the left and the former cemetery office that sits on the right just inside the main Spring Grove Avenue entrance were built in 1863–1867. The chapel, inspired by an English model, was built in 1880. The lovely modern office building, designed by Architekton of Cincinnati and dedicated in 1983, utilizes a geothermal system for heating and cooling and houses a fine reference area for genealogical research. The office staff are most pleasant and helpful and will gladly provide a number of publications about the facility, including a "Self-guided Walking Tour" brochure by Blanche Linden-Ward from which much of the above information was drawn.

As lovely and as historically and architecturally interesting as these major structures are, it is really the grounds, with its lakes and magnificent old trees and its monuments and memorials with the stories they tell (or just enough of a story to pique the visitor's curiosity), that attract the walker. Spring Grove is considered to be the largest private, nonprofit cemetery in the United States and has been designated a national historic landmark.

At last published count, there were 58 trees on the grounds older than 100 years of age. Twenty-five were state champions in size, and two, a two-winged silver bell and a yellowwood (both natives to the southern United States and not to Ohio), were listed as national champions. Shortly after I walked the cemetery in the spring of 1993, a heavy storm damaged many trees, but I assume that most of these giants, which have weathered many previous storms, still stand. A list and map locating these behemoths is available at the office.

The tombstones, statues, and mausoleums are intriguing to study. On my several visits to the cemetery, I found delight in homing in on one or two families or ethnic groups on each visit. Hundreds of Cincinnati's, Ohio's, and the nation's famous person-ages rest beneath the spreading branches of Spring Grove. Thirty-three who fought in the Revolutionary War rest there, and hundreds from each of the succeeding turmoils that have besieged this country have found peace at last beneath the sod of this 150-year-old burying place. Pick your subject: baseball players, Union generals, politicians, industrialists, educators, scientists. Many lie near or in spectacular pieces of cemetery art. Other stones are plain but tell of the life of the people who built southwestern Ohio and the nation. Personal crises, epidemics, conflict, love, grief—it's all there for the reading. The grounds are open to vehicles as well as to pedestrians, but to get the true feel of the social history revealed in the tombstones and monuments, walking is the way to see Spring Grove.

An oasis in a largely urban county of nearly 875,000 residents, Spring Grove, like similar large, rural cemeteries established during the early nineteenth century, is a good stopover and even a nesting site for Neotropical birds. Tom Thomson devotes a full page to Spring Grove in his book, *Birding in Ohio*, a resource on Ohio birds and birding well worth owning and referring to often.

Access

Spring Grove Cemetery lies close to the center of Hamilton County and greater Cincinnati on the west side of Mill Creek. It is reached by taking Mitchell Avenue north from I-75 to Spring Grove Avenue, then turning left and traveling .5 mile to the cemetery entrance on the left. Gates are open from 8 A.M. to 5 P.M. daily. After entering the gate, turn right beyond the gatehouse and park in the lot across the road from the new administration center. This is private property, and visitors are expected to conduct themselves accordingly. There are restrooms in the administration center but nowhere on the grounds. Picnicking is not permitted.

Trail

Begin walking by returning to the entrance drive, turning right, and heading north-northeast on the main entrance road through the underpass. Note that the trail suggested here follows some of the route of the "Self-guided Walking Tour," though in the opposite direction, but for the most part, the routes are different. The hike I describe is considerably longer since you visit the "woodland area" at the upland end of the cemetery—an opportunity to see wildflowers, small mammals, and songbirds and to pass near the cemetery's oldest tree, a giant white oak. An option is suggested if you don't feel up to the climb. All sections are numbered, with numbers often posted on trees near intersections. Keep track of the numbers since this guide will refer to them. The roads are not named, but the main road from the entrance on Spring Grove Avenue to the north gate on Gray Road is referred to as the central avenue and carries a white stripe down its center. Eastern and western cross-cemetery routes are also color coded, but this description does not utilize either.

The first monument that comes into view nearly straight ahead as you walk into the grounds is that of William L. Lytle, one of 37 Civil War generals who were laid to rest at Spring Grove. This stone is a 1915 replacement for an earlier memorial of limestone that was destroyed by acid rain from Mill Creek valley industry. Other family members, including the general's grandfather, a veteran of the French and Indian Wars, are interred in this memorial. The severed column on the monument indicates life cut short; the grieving eagle holding a garland atop the column tells of the patriotic nature of the general's death.

Turn left, with the railroad to the left of the road. On the right, beyond a number of massive, widely spaced monuments to some of the city's most prominent nineteenth-century families, lies Maketewha Lake, one of the many ponds built by Superintendent Strauch. There are a few beds of perennials here and there in the cemetery, but no overload of flower beds, even during the spring and summer, and not a plastic flower in sight. Instead, you see just lovely, natural landscape.

At the first intersection there stands a Corinthian temple as a monument to Ohio's "Fighting McCook's." This Carroll County family of 20 gave 15 of its sons to the Union cause in the Civil War. Seven family members are interred here, including two generals, one officer, and one soldier who all died in the war.

At the McCook monument, turn right, with Willow Lake on the left. This picturesque pond is fed by a lovely falls carrying water from Cascade Lake upslope, all a part of Strauch's plan to give the grounds a natural, parklike quality. A rather recent black granite memorial wall is located here.

The Erckenbrecher monument at the next intersection is one of the few, full-length, cast bronze statues in the cemetery, a semi-reclining, draped female figure in the beaux-arts style. As the road begins to climb, you will see monuments on the hillside to the left, as well as between the road and the lake on the right. Union General Peter John Sullivan's tomb is on the right, and that of Cincinnati Art Museum founder Charles W. West, represented in a life-sized, seated sculpture, is also on the right. Staying with the left fork of the road, you pass under a lovely chinquapin oak as you approach the large Gothic Revival mausoleum of the Dexter family, built in 1869. It looks like it has not been entered for years.

Here you can turn right and continue along the north shore of Geyser Lake, thus rejoining the central avenue at the interment office to return to your car. If you are up to about three times as much walking and some hill climbing, turn left here and continue the steady climb. The tomb of former U.S. Supreme Court Chief Justice Salmon P. Chase is on the left. At the top of this rise, where the road again splits, sits a lovely pink stone that says, "The Caledonian Society of Cincinnati—1892," with the graves of four McLeods clustered nearby. Each tombstone bears the inscription, "native of Scotland."

Here, turn left, with section 43 on the right and 31 on the left. The Hale monument (labeled Hall on the cemetery map) sits on the left at the intersection. A hundred yards further, at the intersection that separates sections 31 and 41 on the left, continue clockwise, following the road to the right in the shade of lovely hardwoods. The tombstones are not as big in this area of the cemetery, but names that have been prominent in Cincinnati for years can still be found along here. Many bear the country of origin of the interred, calling attention to the melting pot nature of Cincinnati, the "Gateway to the West." Most, though, are of northern European descent.

At the intersection between sections 48 and 75 on the left, turn left to climb a hillside again. Continue across the intersection beyond section 72 on the right and 71 on the left. In section 60 on the left you will see a flagpole and a world war veteran burial area downhill to the left. Visible in the distance is another small lake. On the right are many less-pretentious burial sites—flush headstones with ever-

The Burnet mausoleum, near the end of the Spring Grove walk,
is built into the hillside close to Cedar Lake.

greens in between. In another 100 feet, you reach another intersection where an obelisk to Jane Mills is visible ahead. Turn right here to pass alongside the "woodland area" on the left, where there are no graves. This part of the 733 acres is, at this time, reserved for wildflowers and wild creatures. Enjoy their bright colors and blithe spirits.

After huffing and puffing to the next intersection, turn left to travel on the white-striped central avenue of the cemetery. Soon on the left there is a small parking area, some benches, a bird feeder, and a mowed path that leads back into the woodland area. There is a very old redbud tree that guards the entrance to this walking trail.

Leaving this off-road setting, turn left to follow the white-striped road around to the right toward the North Gate entrance. Tombstones here have the twentieth-century look, with the colors and types of stone giving away their origins from places such as Vermont and North Carolina. Toward the end of section 113 on the right stands the national champion water oak tree. Look for it.

Hanging a hard right starts us back toward our trailhead. At a monument just after this turn, there is an inscription that reads, "At evening time it shall be light." As you arc to the right, you will be alongside section 113 until the road splits. Continuing to the right, the section alongside you will change to 100. On the left is section 101, in the middle of which grows the oldest tree in the cemetery, a large white oak. Make a side trip to pay it the homage it is due. Many of our native plants, from skunk cabbage to white oak, have longer life spans than do humans.

At the next junction, where a Voltz monument lies ahead, continue straight across the intersection and continue descending. Large tuliptrees grow on the left, with ivy and juniper on the steep slope to the right. The Pugsley family chose to use an Ohio granite glacial erratic as a grave marker in section 84 on the right, an action that pleased me greatly. After a road comes in from the right, there is a small mausoleum marked John H. Fry cut into the hillside on the left.

Near a huge burr oak tree, the green-striped easterly road joins the one on which you are walking. Curve right, with the boundary fence clearly visible to the left. After passing another burr oak and arriving at the Stone obelisk, turn left, traveling through a mixed forest of native hardwoods and introduced evergreens between sections 47 and 39. In this area of early burials, stop to read some of the nearby stones. One stone in section 47 tells of Peter Fraser, who was born in Flanders, New Jersey, on March 13, 1816, and died by committing suicide in Cincinnati on May 21, 1856. Death at one's own hand is seldom noted on a tombstone. The inscription is no longer very legible, but it reads something like "a citizen for about ten years, a man of integrity, loved and [?] by son, brother and beloved wife." Persons with other surnames are listed on the Fraser obelisk, including one also noted as having been born in Flanders, New Jersey. Wouldn't you like to know the rest of the story?

Continue around section 47 until the Kidd mausoleum comes into view ahead. Jog left, then right, ending up with section 45 on the right and 36 on the left. On the left, there is a large spruce tree, a recently planted burr oak, and an obelisk marking the final resting place of William F. Neff. Could he have been a member of the Neff family of Cincinnati that, in the closing decades of the nineteenth century, speculated on land along Yellow Springs Creek in Greene County, building the spacious Neff House spa near the springs in the area now known as Glen Helen? During my 17 years as director of Glen Helen, I always intended to try to discover more about the Cincinnati Neffs.

On the right, across the road from the Neff graves, sits an interesting, shoulder-high, grey-green stone sphinx atop a stone base. This is the Lawler monument, erected in 1850 by Davis B. Lawler in honor of his parents, Philadelphia-born Matthew Lawler, Esq., and Mrs. Anne Lawler, identified as Matthew's consort. The names of many of Matthew's descendants, including his son, Davis B., and Davis's Berlin, Prussian-born wife, Augusta A. E. Creutz, have been added to the side of this unusual monument—an interesting transference of Egyptian archaeology to America.

After descending the hill past many weeping cherry trees, you can see Geyser Lake straight ahead. The large island is, appropriately, Strauch Island, where Adolph is buried under a modest stone set low to the earth. The beautiful structure on the far left shore is the Neoclassical Fleischmann mausoleum, built in 1913. It was modeled after the Parthenon in Athens and is the final resting place of Charles Louis Fleischmann, well-known yeast manufacturer, and his wife, Henrietta Robinson.

Beyond the interment office and the area reserved for Masons, there is a dramatic bronze statue of a Union soldier that commemorates all Cincinnatians who died in the War between the States. It stands in an intersection almost as if it were in the middle of a small-town square. Its cost of $25,000 was raised by subscription in 1864, a year before the war's end. "The Sentinel," or "Soldier of the Line" as it was called by the artist, was the work of Randolph Rogers, an American then living in Rome, and was the first of many Civil War monuments he designed for locations throughout the North. Spring Grove's version, cast in 1865 by Ferdinand von Muller in Munich, was thus probably the prototype for many that were erected across the land during the decade following the war.

Turn left at "The Sentinel" and begin traveling in a clockwise manner, with Cedar Lake and section 21 to the right and, initially, section 23 to the left. Up the slope in section 23 is a tombstone built like the trunk of an oak tree and set on a piece of limestone that is brimming with fossils, probably Ordovician aged and of local origin. The inscriptions are all in German and are badly weathered. This is the final resting place of Andrew H. Ernst, one of the founders of Spring Grove and an active horticulturist, and for other members of his family who preceded him in death and whose coffins he moved to this location. The entire style of this nineteenth-century funerary art is Germanic, emphasizing death as a natural process. The tombstone was sculpted by Louis Fettweis in the 1840s and is one of my favorites.

Return to the road to continue around section 21. The Burnett mausoleum sits to the left just past another intersection. Just beyond it, to the left of the road, grows a tall ginkgo tree, one of many in this area. Across the road stands a tall larch tree and, in the distance across the lake, a nice stand of bald cypress complete with "knees" along the shore. The close working relationship between the cemetery association and the Cincinnati Horticultural Society in the early years is very visible here.

Leave the right side of the road and explore the area, reading tombstones and monuments as you head west to return to the central avenue and the entrance. There are several tall obelisks surrounded by tombstones, but the most striking areas are those where the graves of hundreds of Union and Confederate soldiers lie in concentric circles, each marked with a flush marble square revealing name and military unit. At the center of each of these areas is an upturned canon barrel. There is also a mounted artillery piece dedicated to "The Unknown" that was added in 1907, more than 40 years after the fighting stopped. Even with the terrible losses of two world wars and many other overseas actions, this century will never fully understand how the Civil War affected our state and nation. About 350,000 Ohio men served in the Civil War, and 35,475 of them died.

Return to the central avenue close to the red granite column and pedestal topped with an allegorical figure and anchor that commemorates the Holenshade family. Imported from Scotland in 1867, it commemorates not just one but many members of the extended family. A left turn onto the road heads us toward the railroad underpass, the buildings, and the parking lot, bringing to a close this exploration into a classic example of the rural cemetery movement. Return often; there is much to see and learn along Spring Grove's quiet roads and peaceful lakes.

Winton Woods Park

Distance: 1¾ miles
Accessibility: Because of terrain and trail surface,
access by physically challenged is impossible.
Facilities: Restrooms, drinking water, boating, fishing,
visitor center, Parcours fitness trail, ball
fields, picnic tables and shelters, riding center
and bridle trails, campground, golf course.

The second largest in size and the most heavily visited of the regional parks operated by the Hamilton County Park District, Winton Woods is also probably the most easily accessible. Begun in 1939 when 904 acres were leased from the United States Department of Agriculture, the park now encompasses 2,375 acres of the upper end of the heavily industrialized Mill Creek valley. The 188-acre flood control impoundment known as Winton Lake is heavily silted, but, nevertheless, it contains some quite natural areas where wildflowers and wild creatures can be seen and enjoyed.

Within the park, Spring Beauty Dell and the Greenbelt area have been designated as state scenic nature preserves. Along with the multiplicity of outdoor recreational opportunities offered, Winton Woods has two hiking trails that together total 1¾ miles. The Kingfisher Trail and the Great Oaks Trail are both of modest difficulty and, together, can be easily walked in less than 2 hours.

Like all of the regional parks of the Hamilton County Park system, possession of an annual vehicle pass or purchase of a daily entry permit is required for entry.

Access

Winton Woods is easily reached from I-275 by turning south on Winton Road and traveling until reaching the park, which the road dissects. Turn west (right) on Valley View Drive to reach the parking lots that serve the Great Oaks and Kingfisher trails.

Trails

The one-mile, self-guided Kingfisher hiking trail begins by a wetland and meanders through an area known as the Greenbelt, a dedicated state nature preserve. The trail takes its name from the large, fish-eating birds of that name that are often seen perched above the nearby Kingfisher Lake, watching for easy prey.

To reach it, park at the Kingfisher picnic area lot located on the north side of Valley View Drive, west of the ranger office and visitor center. The trailhead is at the left rear corner of the lot as you face away from the road. Begin walking north among the bush honeysuckle and multiflora rose. About 100 feet from the trailhead, an interpretive sign above a rotting log talks about the sponge or litter layer of the forest, as typified by the decaying tree seen here. The "consumers" that feed on rotting matter are important in returning nutrients that were tied up in living plants to the soil for reuse.

After crossing a dike that helps create this wetland, the trail reaches a "Y." Turn left to follow the trail in a clockwise direction. You soon reach a boardwalk where a sign reminds visitors that boardwalks are slippery when wet, as indeed they are. The boardwalk is four-feet wide, and it twists and turns along the area that a sign identifies as the Kingfisher wetland. Soon leaving the boardwalk, the trail reaches a sign that attempts to instill in youngsters a sense of wonder.

Along the trail are some tall trees and, in the summer, many beautiful plants of the wet meadow and open field. The ten-foot-tall giant ragweed will be alarming to some. Its pollen, of course, is one of the principal agents causing hay fever in the late summer.

Now surfaced with finely crushed limestone, the trail crosses a small stream on a bridge, beyond which there is a place to sit and observe the natural scene. Alongside the trail there stands a huge green ash tree, perhaps 38 inches in diameter at breast height. A hundred fifty feet further along the trail, a sign draws the hiker's attention to a bush honeysuckle and a multiflora rose, both aliens

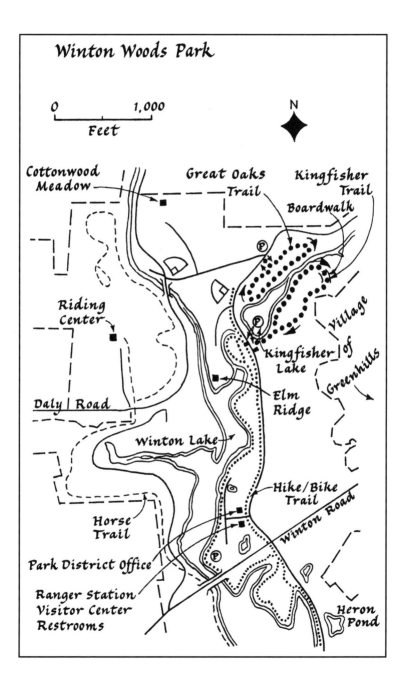

Winton Woods Park

that were imported and have become great nuisance plants. Still paralleling the creek, the trail passes skunk cabbage, pawpaw, black cherry, hackberry, and basswood, the latter two perhaps indicating a relatively high alkalinity in the substrate and/or water. Vines, including poison ivy, are the subject of the next interpretive sign.

Where the trail comes close to the creek, Boy Scouts were performing a bank stabilization project on the day I visited the area. One hundred fifty feet beyond, the trail swings right and climbs 20 steps to return to a boardwalk. Elevated two or three feet above the ground, the boardwalk carries the trail for perhaps 125 feet, spanning small streams that carry runoff to the creek.

"History in the rocks," the sign says as it interprets the Ordovician origin of the bedrock of the area. Beyond the sign is a stream whose course is defined by the presence of multiflora rose bushes.

Now back on the ground, the eight-foot wide, crushed limestone trail here looks as if it often carries as much water as the nearby stream. "Imagine any of these forest trees as a house," the next sign begins as it talks about the creatures, warm and cold blooded, that inhabit the trees. Having followed a stream for many yards, the trail now crosses it over a buried culvert. The need for specific habitat for specific birds is discussed on yet another sign.

The path travels through great thickets of multiflora rose, climbing euonymus, privet, and bush honeysuckle as it continues its return to the parking lot, passing several more signs along the way. Perhaps the most interesting sign explains a nearby sinkhole. A carsonite post points the way to a 20-foot wooden bridge. The trail then turns 90 degrees to the right, passing a hackberry and some invading young pines. With the wetland 75 feet to the right, the trail leads toward the dike to close the loop and carry the hiker back to the parking lot.

The parking lot for the Great Oaks Trail is the one that serves the Walnut Ridge picnic area on the northeast side of Valley View Drive near the west end of the park. Named after the large oak trees found along the trail, the ¾-mile trail also borders the Kingfisher Lake wetland. Moderate in difficulty, it can be easily hiked in less than 1 hour. Because the trail is located close to a busy park road, the sound of traffic is ever present; nonetheless, for a short hike close to home, this trail offers much to see.

The trailhead sign describes the trail route. The gravel trail begins by dropping perhaps 75 feet as it heads to the valley below the road. Overhead are large white oaks, black walnuts, sugar maples, ashes, and other native hardwoods. As the trail reaches a "T" to begin its loop configuration, there is a sign telling of the value of wetlands. Take the trail to the left, moving clockwise, and continue down the slope to the wetland area. The trees overhead here are beech and sugar maple. The trail soon reaches some steps with a handrail.

At the bottom of the steps, follow the gravel trail straight ahead, ignoring the wild cross trails. Eventually the trail turns downstream, clinging to the hillside with timbers on the downhill side to keep it in place. After 100 feet, an interpretive sign talks about Kingfisher Creek and advises you to keep your senses alert for the sounds and sights of nature. Only moments after I read this, a bullfrog began tuning up in the wetland below.

You finally reach the floodplain via the gravel trail, where the tree species change to those normally found in that environment— species such as ash, boxelder, elm, and Ohio buckeye. The trail is now about six feet above the level of the creek, and wild trails, irresistible to youngsters, lead to the stream's edge. As you reach the muddy bottomland, glance up at the hillside and admire the huge white oak that stands about halfway up the slope. Below it are sugar maples and pawpaws.

The trail turns toward the hill near a huge, grossly carved beech tree, then begins its ascent over gravel and waterbars. A number of large sugar maples loom overhead, and here and there are some nice black walnuts. Further up the trail is a group of very large white oak trees, those for which the trail is named. Beyond, the trail follows a terrace perhaps 30 feet downslope from the road. At a pair of large red oaks, a sign relates the natural history of oaks. Other oaks, including several white oaks and white oak hybrids, stand close by. No young oaks are anywhere to be seen, but, of course, since oak seedlings are not shade tolerant, that is to be expected. When these ancient trees do succumb to lightning, disease, pollution, or old age, the tall trees of this hillside will likely become sugar maples, the shade-tolerant species ever present in the understory awaiting its time in the sun.

The trail makes a jog to the left up the slope with some railroad tie steps, then turns right to travel closer to the roadway. This close to the woodland edge, the floor of the forest is mostly dominated by plants like poison ivy and garlic mustard. Another interpretive sign talks about the open area to the left and the purported advantages of woodland edge for some species of wildlife. The open area is growing in fast, much of it being choked by bush honeysuckle.

The trail reaches a service road where 12 steps lead down to the junction with the entry trail. At the "T," a left turn returns the hiker to the parking lot.

Though badly contorted by the hand of man, the nature of things seen along both these trails makes them handy for both recreation and education.

Ohio Brush Creek
Watershed

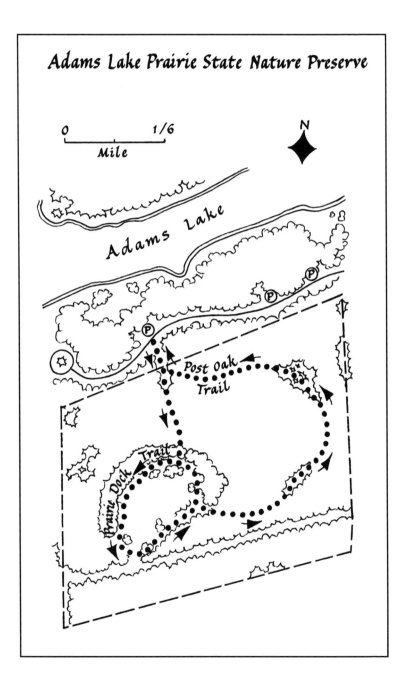

Adams Lake Prairie State Nature Preserve

0   1/6
Mile

N

Adams Lake

Post Oak Trail

Prairie Dock Trail

Adams Lake Prairie
State Nature Preserve

Distance: ¾ mile
Accessibility: Slope, trail surface, and steps make access
by physically challenged nearly impossible.
Facilities: Picnic tables, grills, and restrooms
available in adjacent state park.

The unglaciated hills of Adams County might seem like the least likely place for you to come upon prairie, yet, tucked in here and there on the hillsides in the Ohio Brush Creek watershed are patches of native prairie grasses and forbs (a term botanists use for the nongrasslike plants of the prairie). The grasses of these dry or xeric prairies are, for the most part, the same species that would be found on the short-grass prairies hundreds of miles west of Ohio: little bluestem, side-oats grama, and triple-awn grass.

Exactly how these prairies came into existence in this locality is not clear, but most scientists believe that the prairie plants here are relics from grassland communities that existed in the area during an earlier warm, dry period. They appear to thrive on these hillside locations because of the underlying bedrock of calcareous shale. This material, known as the Crab Orchard Shale, was derived from mud and silts deposited at the bottom of an ancient sea more than 455 million years ago. It is easily eroded, and, once cleared of the forest that probably existed on it at the time of settlement, it quickly lost what topsoil did exist. Soon useless as cropland, it was abandoned by farmers and left to erode. The oaks and hickories growing nearby were unable to get a foothold on the bare shale, however junipers as well as many prairie plants were able to do so. These species thrive in the open sun and on the very thin alkaline soil. Even after so many years of abandonment, not many hardwoods have returned, because severe erosion continues to allow no buildup of topsoil. Among the few woody species that can make it on the calcareous substrate are, in addition to the juniper, shrubby St. John's-wort, blue ash, Carolina buckthorn, ninebark, and shingle and blackjack oaks.

The prairie adjacent to Adams Lake State Park was called to the attention of the Department of Natural Resources in the late 1960s by the late Dr. E. Lucy Braun of the University of Cincinnati. Braun, a world-renowned plant ecologist, had spent much of her life studying the vegetation of Adams County. Shortly after the Division of Natural Areas and Preserves was created, the 25.8-acre tract was acquired and dedicated as a state nature preserve. There are some woodland and prairie flowers in bloom from spring through frost, but the spectacular display occurs after mid-July when the prairie colors are at their peak.

Management of the area includes the removal of junipers and some of the hardwoods that occasionally do get a foothold along the prairie margin. Periodic prescribed burning may also be used to control the invasion of woody plants in the xeric prairie area.

An interesting inhabitant of this preserve is the red mound-builder ant. Large colonies of this mound-building species are seen throughout the xeric prairie. During the summer, these mounds may contain as many as 100,000 workers in elaborate tunnel systems below ground. Considered to be aggressive ants, they feed indiscriminately on vegetable and animal material. They have powerful mandibles and secrete formic acid when attacking. They normally will not bother humans unless their mound is disturbed, but it is a good idea not to stand close to one of their mounds for an extended length of time. Their movement can be observed with a pair of close-focusing binoculars.

The uncommon Edwards' hairstreak butterfly has been found at this preserve. Although its eggs are known to be laid under next year's buds or on rough twigs of its host plants, fully grown larvae have been found in mound-builder ant nests at the base of oaks such as those found at Adams Lake Prairie. As an adult, this butterfly species is known to nectar on sweet clover, an alien biennial planted by farmers as a forage crop, which is found in this prairie. This legume is considered an undesirable invader in the preserve, and efforts are made to control it.

*As ants excavate a massive undergound system of tunnels
and chambers, they create these conical-shaped mounds.*

A booklet about the natural history of this preserve is available
from the ODNR Division of Natural Areas and Preserves.

Access

Located in Tiffin Township in the central part of Adams County, this
preserve is reached by traveling 1.5 miles north from West Union
(the county seat) on OH 41 to the entrance of Adams Lake State Park
on the west (left) side of the highway. The trailhead is on the south
side of the park road opposite a parking lot and picnic area, .5 mile
from the entrance.

Trails

A bulletin board at the trailhead posts a map of the trails. There are two, the Prairie Dock Trail and the Post Oak Trail. They interconnect, so it is easy to walk them both together. I suggest going directly upslope to where the Prairie Dock Trail makes a loop around the prairie. Turn right at that intersection, where there are several post oak trees, interesting because of their crosslike leaf shape. Even if the year has been dry and few have bloomed, the prairie dock for which this trail is named will be visible throughout the year because of its large, docklike leaves. Walking the trail counterclockwise will lead you past a great variety of prairie plants, nearly all easily seen and photographed from the trail. In midsummer, the lavender of bergamot and several species of blazingstar complements the yellow of prairie dock, whorled rosinweed, tall coreopsis, and sunflowers. Butterfly weed makes an orange splash that draws great-spangled fritillaries and other butterflies to drink its nectar through much of June and July. As frost nears, the subtle violet hue of stiff gentian celebrates the end of another growing season.

On the lower side of the loop, the trail surface is natural, but as it rises to return along the top of the slope, boardwalk makes the trail passable in all but the rainiest of times.

Four-fifths of the way around the Prairie Dock Trail, take the Post Oak Trail that takes off to the right. It goes uphill, downhill, and across several footbridges as it passes through typical second-growth eastern hardwood forest. Oak and hickory are joined by a variety of species, including sassafras, ash, and black walnut. The vernal flora is typical of southern Ohio woodland. Among other species, watch for the delicate, violet wood-sorrel close to the trail. In early June, the tobaccolike basal leaves of American columbo will direct the hiker's attention to that unusually tall, green-flowered biennial of the gentian family growing in the woods close to the prairie. The Post Oak Trail ends when it joins the main trail about 50 feet above the bulletin board and parking lot.

Buzzardroost Rock

Distance: 4½ miles round-trip
Accessibility: Because of the rugged terrain,
access by physically challenged not possible.
Facilities: None.

The first known official report of Split Rock, as Buzzardroost Rock was then called, is in a geologic summary dated 1838 by John Locke. More than likely, this high dolomite projection, surrounded on three sides by 75-foot-high cliffs, was known and used by pre-Columbian Native Americans. Situated 500 feet above the valley below, it would have made an ideal lookout or ceremonial site.

Buzzardroost Rock is located on the east side of Ohio Brush Creek in the area of the state with the greatest relief. Greenbriar Ridge, a wooded hill capped with Mississippian-aged Berea sandstone and lying to the south of Buzzardroost Rock, has an elevation of 1,265 feet. The normal elevation of Ohio Brush Creek below Buzzardroost Rock is 485 feet.

Prior to the Pleistocene era, which began 1,500,000 years ago, Buzzardroost Rock was part of an east-west ridge that extended across what is now the valley of Ohio Brush Creek. This ridge formed the southern divide for a northeast-flowing stream, possibly a tributary of the preglacial, north-flowing Teays River. Another tributary, probably of the same river system, flowed south from the ridge in the valley now occupied by Ohio Brush Creek and the Ohio River east of the mouth of Ohio Brush Creek.

The present-day Ohio Brush Creek valley was formed and Buzzardroost Rock exposed when the north-flowing stream system was blocked by the advance of an ice sheet. Upon melting, the glacier released a huge volume of water that formed a lake, which finally rose to a cull in the ridge. The water then cut through the cull eventually to become a part of the Ohio River system.

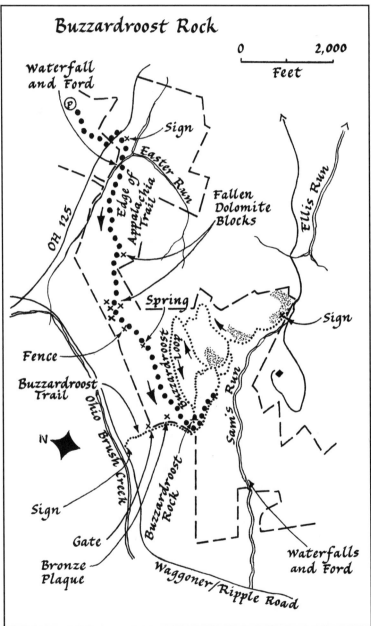

Buzzardroost Rock

A monolith, Buzzardroost Rock is composed of the massive Peebles dolomite of Silurian age. Though often honeycombed on the surface, this rock is well cemented and does not weather rapidly or crumble away. Below it, the well-bedded and cross-bedded Bisher dolomite, which is less resistant to breakup, is exposed. The bedrock beneath the dolomite that is responsible for the gently sloping hillside is the calcareous Crab Orchard shale. The next strata down is Brassfield limestone, a stone that is quarried to make cement elsewhere in Ohio. Below it you finally reach Richmond limestone and shale.

These Silurian-age rocks are all calcareous. The carboniferous, Devonian-age Ohio black shale lies on top of the Peebles formation on the hill above Buzzardroost Rock; thus, plants that do well on acidic soils thrive there, and those that do well on more neutral or alkaline soils live in pockets in the dolomite and on the slopes below.

Four floristic elements influence the plant life that can be seen at Buzzardroost Rock: *prairie species* related to a postglacial xerothermic period, *Appalachian species* related to the nonglaciated acidic soils above the promontory, *Southern species* related to the earlier continuity of the area with the land south of the present-day Ohio River, and the *woodland species* of southwestern Ohio. More than 60 threatened and endangered plant species are found in Adams County, the second-largest number of any county in Ohio

The Nature Conservancy and the Cincinnati Museum of Natural History began acquiring land in this area in 1958. It is now included in a much larger Edge of Appalachia Preserve encompassing over 11,000 acres of land along Ohio Brush Creek. They jointly manage it as a single bioreserve. The original Buzzardroost Rock area, where this trail is located, is dedicated to the memory of Cincinnati siblings, Christian and Emma Goetz, who gave generously toward the establishment of the Adams County preserves.

Explore the beauty of this very special place, staying aware that you are the guest of the Museum and the Conservancy and of unborn generations of Ohioans who will want it to be the same treasure you have found when it is their time to explore.

Access

Located approximately 7 miles southeast of the county seat—the village of West Union—Buzzardroost Rock is in Brush Creek Township of Adams County. There is only one public trail leading into it, which begins at a small parking lot on Township Road 5. This road is the old route of the present-day OH 125 that runs just east of Ohio Brush Creek on the north side of the new highway. To reach it, travel east on OH 125 from West Union. Immediately after crossing the Ohio Brush Creek bridge, turn left (opposite the entrance to Waggoner-Ripple Road). This old road will turn east almost immediately, paralleling OH 125. Near the highest point on the road, there is a small parking area on the right (south) side of the road. It may not be mowed and might be a little trashy. Put all valuables out of sight and lock the car. The entrance to the trail is off the far right corner of the lot. A "Buzzardroost Rock—Christian and Emma Goetz Preserve" sign stands about 40 feet down the trail.

Trail

The trail drops immediately to cross OH 125. Be especially cautious as drivers tend to speed down this straight stretch of highway. The forest cover is a mixture of red cedars and young hardwoods as the trail drops to the floodplain of Easter Run. Downstream from the bridge, Easter Falls, formed by the resistant layers of Brassfield limestone, is visible below. The shale and limestone of the Richmond formation are visible on down this lively creek.

The trail turns left, heading up the gentle slope where the substrate is Crab Orchard shale. Lots of junipers and, in the summer, prairie wildflowers grow by the path. Because there is little humus on the surface of this easily eroded soil, the plants tend to look undernourished and under watered. The rusty-colored soil is caused by the iron impurities in the calcareous shale. The area is often very wet on the surface because the shale is impervious, so after a rain, water moves sideways rather than into the soil, running down the hillside.

After climbing perhaps ¼ mile, the trail turns right to follow the contour of the hillside in a counterclockwise manner. When there

The observation platform on Buzzardroost Rock
overlooks the Ohio Brush Creek valley.

are no leaves on the trees, it's possible to look north across OH 125 and see Teakettle Rock, another weathered Peebles dolomite promontory. Soon, huge blocks of dolomite that have fallen from the cliff upslope are seen beside the trail—blocks as large as a two-car garage. One has been measured at 34' x 61' x 25' and was estimated to weigh 4,500 tons. For the next few minutes, the trail is almost level as it continues around the hillside. The sweet soil along here produces a good show of spring wildflowers.

Beyond, the trail passes through an area that not too long ago was farmed. The former pasture and cultivated fields of the Baldwin farm have all but disappeared beneath boxelder, locust, and other pioneer species. When I passed through this area at about noon one August day, I flushed a large flock of wild turkey.

After passing by the old farm area, the trail begins to climb once more. It was along here that the old trail coming up from Waggoner-Ripple Road used to join this trail. That route has been closed for many years. At one time, there was a National Park Service natural landmark monument attached to a block of dolomite not far down the slope.

Below Buzzardroost Rock, which is visible from beneath only when the leaves have fallen, there are more slump blocks. The trail swings hard to the left to begin moving gradually up the left bank of Sam's Run ravine.

With waterbars and switchbacks, the ascent gets steeper as the trail swings left toward the summit of the hill behind the Rock. Soon outwash of Ohio black shale from up the hill is visible on the trail. Take shorter and slower steps, and soon the top will come into view. It is not necessary to go clear to the summit, which is more than 80 feet higher than the Rock. At an intersection where a trail goes straight ahead and another bends to the right, go left. Once among the pines, deerberries, greenbrier, sassafras, and chestnut oaks, you are above the promontory. Cross a ravine and head west-southwest downhill. The trail runs along the left of the ridge, occasionally dropping below the shale. Climbing again, the vegetation changes noticeably, and the shale is dramatically visible underfoot. Due west about 40 feet down the slope is the wooden platform atop Buzzardroost Rock. As you approach it, you can see the red iron oxide that "bleeds" from the shale and stains the cliff faces of this area.

Wow! What a view there is from here! Stay on the platform; do not be tempted to explore the cliff edges. Look carefully at the plants that bloom on the rim of the Rock just beyond the rail. They are dry prairie species: cylindric and scaly blazingstars, sunflowers, nodding onion, whorled milkweed, several goldenrods, side-oats grama grass, little bluestem, long-leaved bluets, and many more. The late world-renowned Cincinnati botanist, Dr. E. Lucy Braun, recorded more than 30 prairie species on the promontory back in the twenties.

As I stood admiring the view, several tiger and spicebush swallowtail butterflies dropped in to feed on the milkweed and blazingstar. Even though the white flowers of whorled milkweed are inconspicuous, the swallowtails easily find them for a drink of sweet nectar.

I spent 45 minutes on the Rock that hot August afternoon. A gentle breeze kept me cool, and I was exhilarated by the beauty of the place. I could have spent much more time and discovered something of interest each moment. I consider myself privileged beyond belief to have visited this very special place many times over during the last 40 years. I hope others who continue to do so will join me in seeing that it remains for those who follow to know and cherish.

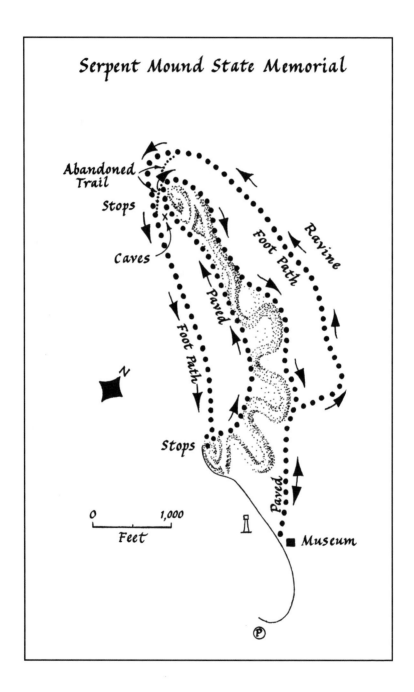

Serpent Mound State Memorial

Abandoned Trail

Stops

Caves

Ravine

Foot Path

Paved

N

Foot Path

Stops

Paved

0 — 1,000
Feet

Museum

(P)

Serpent Mound
State Memorial

Distance: 1 mile
Accessibility: Paved trail on bluff readily accessible by
physically challenged. Trail below bluff edge inaccessible.
Facilities: Picnic shelter and tables, museum,
gift shop, restrooms, drinking water.

I ts picture is probably in every archaeology textbook or illustrated encyclopedia written in the last century. It was illustrated
before cameras were invented, and after they were, it became a
popular subject with the owner of every stereopticon. It's been
studied since the mid-1800s, yet uncertainty as to who built it and
why remains. I'm talking, of course, about the Serpent Mound of
Adams County, considered to be the largest and finest serpent effigy
in North America.

The Serpent Mound was first surveyed by Ephraim Squire and
Edwin Davis of Chillicothe in 1846. Publication of their map and
description in *Ancient Monuments of the Mississippi Valley* in 1848
brought the attention of many people throughout the United States
to it. One such person was Frederick Ward Putnam of Harvard's
Peabody Museum. After visiting the site in 1885, he became so
concerned that it would be destroyed by plowing that he purchased
the mound in Harvard's name. Beginning in 1886, Putnam spent
three years excavating the effigy and other nearby conical mounds.
In 1900, Harvard turned the site over to the Ohio (Archaeological
and) Historical Society, which has managed it ever since.

Since 1967, the society has operated a small museum on the site.
Exhibits illustrate various interpretations of the effigy's form, the
processes believed to have been used in constructing the effigy, the
culture of the Adena and Fort Ancient peoples, and the unique geology
of the Serpent Mound area. There has been an observation tower from

which to view the effigy on site for nearly a century. In 1964, the Serpent Mound was designated a national historic landmark.

Access

Serpent Mound is on a bluff on the east bank of Ohio Brush Creek, in Bratton Township on the northern edge of Adams County. It is easily reached by driving 3.6 miles west on OH 73 from its intersection with OH 41 at Locust Grove.

Except for members of the Ohio Historical Society, there is a small entry fee to the grounds. From April through mid-May, the grounds are open from 10 A.M. to 7 P.M. on Saturdays and Sundays only, and the museum is open from 10 A.M. until 5 P.M. the same days. From Memorial Day weekend through Labor Day, the grounds are open from 9:30 A.M. to 8 P.M. every day, and the museum, from 9:30 A.M. to 5 P.M. After Labor Day and through October, the hours and days are the same as before Memorial Day. The area is closed during the balance of the year.

Trails

To gain some knowledge about Serpent Mound, you will want to start with a visit to the museum. From there, a climb to the observation tower provides an overview of the area and a good vantage point for pictures. Use a wide-angle lens on a single lens reflex or the wide-angle setting on a point-and-shoot camera. The shadows of a late afternoon sun make the effigy more visible in your pictures. The head of the serpent is in the distance, at the end of the open lawn; the coiled tail, off to the left.

Leave the tower, going toward the serpent head on the black-top to the right of the effigy. Two hundred feet beyond the tower and 75 feet to the right of the trail, a sign at an opening in the woods indicates the entrance to a hiking trail. Head down that trail. With dying red cedars in the understory, the north-facing hillside is covered with young mixed mesophytic forest. As expected, the trees and shrubs that do well on limy soils are prominent in the mix. After dropping for about 50 feet, the trail turns left, following the hillside counterclockwise. The trail is not very well cut out of the slope, and

*Some people believe that the builders of the Serpent Mound
may have patterned it after the black rat snack, a large species
found in the area which often raids birds' nests to eat eggs.*

cedar logs have been laid along the downhill side to better define it.

A ravine to the right carries a small stream toward Ohio Brush
creek. The hillside has lots of pawpaw trees, indicating a springy
environment. After dropping ever so slightly, and following the hillside for a couple hundred feet, the trail makes a split, with the right
fork continuing on down to the creek and the left heading upward
toward the bluff near the head of the serpent. Take the left trail uphill.

A 75-foot climb up a broad gravel trail with widely spaced
waterbars brings you to a point where there is a rocky overhang
above. There are also cliffs downslope to the right, and it looks as
if at one time there was a trail in that direction. Our trail turns solidly
to the left and begins an ascent of perhaps another 30 feet. The
groundcover myrtle is probably evidence of an attempt to slow down
erosion on this steep hillside. A cable to the right of the trail serves
as a temporary handrail, then a wooden handrail appears just before
the trail breaks out on top at the overlook in front of the mouth of
the serpent. In midsummer, the lavender-colored prairie plant called

wild petunia blooms profusely in the mowed lawn here. It normally is a plant of one to two feet in height, but it is often seen in this part of Ohio in prairie cemeteries or church lawns in full bloom even though it has been mowed to one and one-half inches.

What does the head of the serpent look like to you? A snake with a fully opened mouth? A black rat snake about to eat a bird's egg? A snake about to eat a frog? You can accept one of the many professional evaluations or make up one of your own.

Return down the steps to the trail to the creek and continue following it around the base of the hill to the left. The nature trail drops over eight steps to the floodplain, which, of course, may be underwater and impassable. In the summer, lots of floodplain species attractive to butterflies bloom here. Ignore the wild paths up the hillside and continue around the base of the hill, passing the point from which a trail once traveled to the serpent's head from this side. There are shallow caves in the soft dolomite halfway up the slope. The trail climbs the hill to just below them, then starts back downhill toward the floodplain. As the trail nears the bottom, a trail goes left back up to the cliffs. Instead, go on to the floodplain trail where, after 100 feet, the trail will rise slightly, then climb eleven steps to just below the soft dolomite. Traveling now on the rocky talus slope, the trail eventually takes a left turn up the slope. After 100 feet of huffing and puffing, you arrive above the cliff's edge close to the coiled tail of the serpent. Fifty feet beyond the edge of the woods is the blacktop path. Turn right, passing a rock wall and rail, to pick up a path to the left that leads to steps up and over the serpent's tail. Pause atop the tail for a picture or two; then take the blacktop path along the left side of the "green" back to the serpent's head. Return to the museum, restrooms, and your vehicle via the path on the other side of the serpent.

Visit this special place often. The spring wildflowers along the nature trail are lovely in May, and the hues of autumn are extraordinary from the overlook where you can look down on the trees. Give some thought as to why you think the earthworks was built. Perhaps it had no great symbolic meaning but was built simply as an expression of pure art.

Scioto Brush Creek Watershed

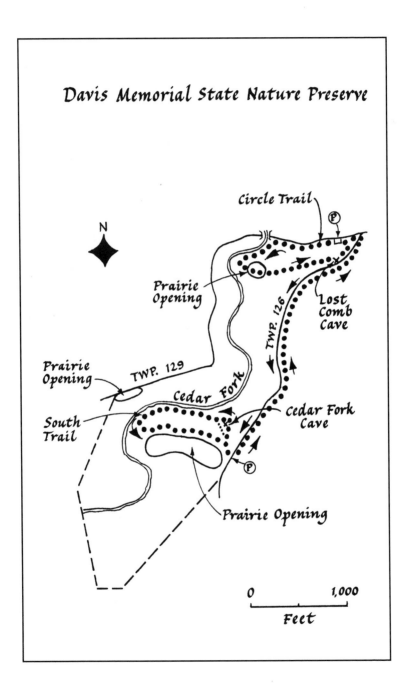

Davis Memorial State Nature Preserve

Circle Trail

Prairie Opening

TWP. 126

Lost Comb Cave

Prairie Opening

TWP. 129

Cedar Fork

South Trail

Cedar Fork Cave

Prairie Opening

0   1,000

Feet

Davis Memorial
State Nature Preserve

Distance: Two trails totaling ¾ mile
Accessibility: Because of the extremely rugged terrain,
access by the physically challenged
is not possible.
Facilities: None.

Never heard of the Mineral Springs area of Ohio? Not many Ohioans have. For Ohio naturalists, however, its fame goes clear back to 1928. It was then that the late Dr. E. Lucy Braun of Cincinnati published a small booklet entitled *Vegetation of the Mineral Springs Area of Adams County, Ohio.* Dr. Braun, a native of Cincinnati, received her M.A. in geology, and, in 1914, her Ph.D. in botany, both from the University of Cincinnati. She was indomitable in her fieldwork on the deciduous forests of southern Ohio and the southern Appalachian Mountains. In 1950, she published *Deciduous Forests of Eastern North America,* the result of 26 years of research and 65,000 miles of travel.

But it was her "Mineral Springs" publication that brought to many Ohio naturalists knowledge of the truly unique habitats of Adams County: arbor vitae–lined gorges, prairie openings, cedar glades, and much more. The publication got its name from the tiny community of Mineral Springs located four miles south of Davis Memorial on Meigs Township Road 126.

By the 1920s, however, the Mineral Springs area of Ohio was not pristine countryside full of virgin forest. Far from it—that part of Ohio had been open for settlement since 1784 when the state of Virginia appropriated back from the federal government land they had earlier ceded in order to satisfy claims of soldiers who had fought in the Revolution. Lying close to the Ohio River, with cheap access by flatboat, it was some of the first lands in the Virginia Military District to be settled.

By 1928, much of the tillable land was worn out, and the timber was gone. Red cedars were invading the potato patches and pastures, and country boys were heading for the city. Where it was easy to reach by wagon or rail, the Peebles dolomite was being quarried. A look at the halftones in Braun's book will show just how worn out the land was.

In 1967, at the urging of some Cincinnati members of The Nature Conservancy, 88 acres of the land that had been in Braun's Mineral Springs study was donated to the people of Ohio and the Ohio Historical Society in honor of the late chairman of the board of directors of Davon, Inc., Edwin H. Davis (1888–1960). It became officially known as Edwin H. Davis State Memorial. In 1993, under an agreement between the Historical Society and the Department of Natural Resources, management was turned over to the Division of Natural Areas and Preserves and the name changed to Davis Memorial State Nature Preserve.

Davis Memorial differs from preserves elsewhere in Adams County in some interesting and important ways. First, it lies in the watershed of Scioto Brush Creek, a tributary of the Scioto River, so it may contain species not found in the Ohio Brush Creek watershed where the other preserves are located. It is especially important, however, because of Dr. Braun's early studies here. Her research provides us with "baseline" data gathered from the area nearly 70 years ago. This circumstance is very unusual in the world of plant science and it provides a means of comparing what is there now with what grew there in the past.

Stroll along the trails of this very special place in company with the indomitable spirit of Lucy Braun (and, in all likelihood, her world-renowned macrolepidopterist sister, Emily Braun).

Access

Travel east from Cincinnati or west from US 23 on OH 32 to the vicinity of Peebles. There, take Steam Furnace Road .4 mile south to Township Road 129, Davis Memorial Road. Turn east (left) and go

Sullivantia, named for nineteenth-century amateur botanist William Starling Sullivant, grows on the moist Peebles dolomite cliffs of Davis Memorial State Nature Preserve.

about 2.7 miles to where you will find a parking area and preserve sign on the right side of the road. The township is Meigs, and the county, Adams. The Buckeye Trail passes through the preserve. The area is a registered national natural landmark.

Trails

There are two loop trails into the preserve. They can be connected by traveling the blue-blazed Buckeye Trail, but I suggest parking at the north entrance and using Township Road 126 on the eastern edge of the preserve to connect with the south trail. In the summer, wildlfowers, birds, butterflies and beetles will be plentiful along this quiet dirt road. A self-guided nature trail brochure has been available in the past but may not be now. Not all the trail marker posts are readily found.

Start the north (Circle) Trail by passing behind the kiosk and turning right (west), walking parallel to the road and toward the creek. The trail crosses a small footbridge over a tiny tributary of Cedar Fork. The hillside to the left is covered with wildflowers in the spring. Redbud and arrow-wood are among the understory trees along here, and witch hazel, from which the astringent of the same name is extracted, grows in the shrub layer. The small shrub, leatherwood, is also known to grow along here.

After it passes a sign that warns of the potential for high water on the floodplain, the trail turns left. Almost immediately, it moves to the base of the dolomite cliffs, so neatly cut away by the action of the stream on freshly exposed bedrock. The Silurian-age Peebles dolomite of Adams County is considered by many to be the same formation as the Cedarville dolomite further upstate. The first plants to grow on the exposed rock in the moist environment of this valley are algae, liverworts, and lichens. These are less likely to grow on the faces of the high dolomite cliffs and promontories of the Edge of Appalachia Preserve area along Ohio Brush Creek, though, because of the direct exposure of these sites to the sun. As the pioneer plants create a bit of humus in crevices and rock pockets, walking fern, purple cliffbreak, bulblet fern, and other plants take hold. These cliff faces are also favorable habitat for the rare rock plant, Sullivantia, named for early Ohio botanist William Starling Sullivant, who discovered the species.

In the forest growing on the dolomite, look for several species of oak, sugar maple, and tuliptree, a member of the magnolia family. The shrubs wild hydrangea and wild gooseberry both grow in the gorge along this section of the trail, as does the small tree, blackhaw. Black walnut, sycamore, and basswood, all floodplain species, occur in the bottomland between here and the road.

Ahead and on the top of the dolomite cliff is a grove of native arbor vitae or white cedar, a native conifer restricted in nature to alkaline soils. Normally found in colder climates, this species has probably survived here since the Ice Age when glaciers came near this area. Its distribution in Ohio is limited to cool, microclimatic areas like this, and to the fen known as Cedar Bog in Champaign County. We might speculate that Cedar Fork was named for these "white cedars" and not for the junipers (red cedars) that invaded the worn-out fields of the area.

Still on the floodplain, there is a stand of pawpaw trees, some ninebark shrubs with their peeling bark (also found at Cedar Bog), some bladdernut trees with their odd, inflated seed capsules in the fall, and spicebush, the food required by the larvae of spicebush swallowtails. Look for this butterfly and for tiger swallowtails "puddling" on a wet sandbar or a dirt road after a shower. The distinctive zebra swallowtail is often seen in these woods, where its larvae use the leaves of pawpaw. I have seen them in late April nectaring on the blossoms of long-spurred violets.

Now with cliffs on the right side of the stream, the trail climbs out of the streambed on the left. If you are tempted to walk over to the edge of the clifftop, be careful. The trail is now on top of the Peebles dolomite on a terrace of sorts. The cliff to the left is of Greenfield dolomite, which lies above the Peebles strata. It tends to weather in layers, ending up looking like a stone wall.

Still on dolomite-derived soils, the canopy includes chinquapin oak, the understory is filled with redbud, and in among them all stands overtopped red cedars left from when this land was reverting from field. On a rocky promontory a short ways up the slope, now all but crowded out, are prairie plants such as hoary puccoon, tall larkspur, and flowering spurge.

Still rising, the trail is now on soil derived from Ohio black shale. The oaks are scarlet, white, black, and chestnut, and sassafras appears. There are fewer red cedars, and in the understory, redbud has been mostly replaced by dogwood. On the forest floor are blueberry and huckleberry—a classic oak-blueberry association. Further down the trail, the forest changes to scrub and Virginia pine. This is a natural second-growth stand. It will be interesting to see if pine or oak persists on these acidic soil ridges if climatic warming continues. As the trail drops downhill, it returns to more alkaline soils and the trees, shrubs, and herbaceous plants that do well on it.

The trail circles close to the road, arcing back toward the kiosk. There is a small outcrop of layered Greenfield dolomite with an opening at its base. This hole drains a sinkhole in the dolomite on the other side of the road. Where the trail reaches the back of the kiosk, there has for many years been a patch of 30-foot-tall large cane. Canebrakes, once common in the south, are said to have occurred as far north as southern Ohio, Indiana, and Illinois. This patch may have been planted here, or it may be one of the northernmost naturally occurring canebrakes.

Now walk the .5 mile east on Township Road 129 and then down Township Road 126 to where the South Trail begins. Grayheaded coneflower, rose-pink, yellow partridge pea, feverwort, butterfly weed, cup plant, whorled rosin-weed, flowering spurge, and other prairie wildflowers grow along the side of this road.

The South Trail comes up on the right side of the road and is not labeled. Two hundred feet in from the road, take the right fork heading toward the creek. It looks like the topsoil may have been removed here as part of a logging operation. Perhaps a portable sawmill sat here. The trees making it here now—scrub pine, red cedar, redbud, and others—are all species that can tolerate alkalinity. I flushed a ruffed grouse from this area on one late summer visit.

After passing exposed Greenfield dolomite and prairie flowers, the trail reaches the top of the Greenfield dolomite. On downslope, a side trail leads to a young solution cave, Cedar Cave. This small cave has two entrances and very small stalactites hanging overhead. The cave has been formed by rainwater made acidic by leaves and other humus flowing into natural cracks or joints in the bedrock, slowly to dissolve away the alkaline rock. In Cedar Cave, the ceiling is Greenfield dolomite, and the floor, Peebles dolomite. Caves and cave resources are protected by law. Please take away only photos and memories.

Back up on the high ground, the trail continues counterclockwise, passing through a mixed hardwood forest with lots of large sugar maple trees on the slope. Tall sycamores grow along the stream in the valley below.

Where the stream makes a large bend and you are looking south-southwest (where a #15 marker may still exist), look across the valley to where a minor fault is visible in the bedrock behind a three-trunked cedar and, when the water is clear, in the streambed below. A short distance upstream, the small valley visible across the creek marks a fault line where there has been nearly 35 feet of displacement, bringing the Greenfield and the Peebles dolomites side by side. The Greenfield on the east is depressed in relation to the massive Peebles, which forms the high promontory on the west. This fault line is believed to extend at least six miles, and the fault thought to be the largest in the area.

Continuing to the left, the trail makes a rigorous climb up an eroded valley to close the south loop. Return to your car via the road. Not far away, the bedrock is being blasted apart, crushed and hauled away, erasing forever the stories that might be read in the rock and on the land. Thanks to the associates of Edwin Davis, this preserve should always be here for those who would learn new lessons.

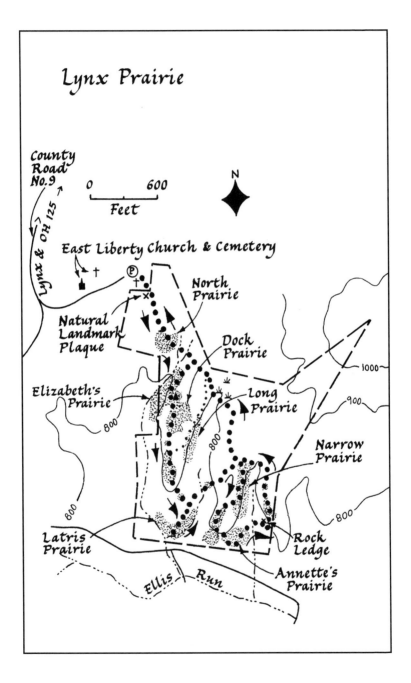

Lynx Prairie

County Road No. 9

Lynx & OH 125

0   600
Feet

N

East Liberty Church & Cemetery

℗

North Prairie

Natural Landmark Plaque

Dock Prairie

Elizabeth's Prairie

Long Prairie

800

800

1000

900

Narrow Prairie

800

Latris Prairie

Rock Ledge

Annette's Prairie

Ellis Run

Lynx Prairie
Preserve

Distance: 1 mile
Accessibility: Rough terrain makes access by
physically challenged virtually impossible.
Facilities: None.

My first visit to the prairie openings around the Adams County town of Lynx was in the late spring of 1949 on a college plant ecology field trip. My field notes refer to them as "cat" prairies, a term I have never heard anywhere else. Perhaps Professor Wolfe dubbed them that because of the nearby village of Lynx.

It took a long time for me to accept the fact that these acre or less patches of grasses and forbs on the worn-out fields of Ohio's poorest county were, in fact, prairies. How could a cowboy on horseback come across one of these? There was hardly enough room for one horse let alone "a thundering herd coming out of a cloud of dust." I had plunked down enough thin dimes for Saturday afternoon serials at the local movie house to know what a prairie looked like. Tom Mix wouldn't be caught dead in an Adams County prairie.

In the nearly half century since I first saw shooting star, Indian paintbrush, hoary puccoon, and yellow-star grass in bloom among the short, green shoots of little bluestem and side-oats grama on "cat prairies" of southern Ohio, I have seen grasslands of all sizes on two continents. Yet, nothing gives me quite the thrill that I get when, spring, summer, or fall, I discover a flower that is an old friend or one I have never seen before in one of these prairies.

Essentially these grasslands are relics of an earlier time when the climate of the interior part of North America was warmer and drier. The prairies spread eastward to wherever soil and exposure gave advantage to grasses and forbs over forest. Analysis of Ohio peat bogs shows that such a xerothermic period brought prairie species into western Ohio perhaps 3,000–5,000 years ago. A return to a cooler, more moist climate resulted in reexpansion of forests into most of Ohio. Here, on the hillsides and clifftops of this part of Ohio where shallow soils overlay porous, Silurian-age dolomite, conditions were not conducive to the growth of trees. But the long-lived, deep-rooted, fire- and drought-resistant perennial plants of the prairies could survive and grow, so the "cat prairies" remained.

There are other places in Ohio with outcrops or clifftops where shallow soil exists over limestone or dolomite. Many, like Glen Helen and Stillwater Prairie Reserve, have small populations of some prairie plants. But here, where the glaciers never scraped the land flat, the dolomites are exposed around the hillsides, thus prairie openings at essentially the same elevation strung around the hillsides south of Lynx.

In 1959, at the urging of the late Dr. E. Lucy Braun of the University of Cincinnati Department of Botany, the brand-new Ohio Chapter of The Nature Conservancy purchased the 53-acre tract now known as Lynx Prairie. It was soon transferred to the Cincinnati Museum of Natural History for care. Now, nearly four decades later, it is a unit of the extensive Edge of Appalachia BioReserve, jointly owned and managed by the conservancy and the museum. At least 66 plant species considered to be threatened or endangered in Ohio are known to grow in Adams County, and the management of the prairie openings has helped spawn the young science of restoration management.

A walk on the trail through Lynx Prairie is very special. The hike will help those who love the out-of-doors learn about the incredible diversity of life that makes up this earth—not just the biodiversity of the tropical rainforests of the southern hemisphere that we hear so much about, but of special places close to home.

Access

Brush Creek Township in Adams County is the site of the small village of Lynx. The preserve is reached by traveling .3 mile south from OH 125 on Tulip Road to the East Liberty Church driveway,

The large arrowlike leaves to the left of the trail belong to prairie dock, a perennial that has sunflowerlike blossoms on tall stalks in midsummer.

then about .1 mile to the back end of the cemetery. The entrance to the preserve is via a pass-through in a fence at the south side of the old section of the cemetery that lies to the south of the drive. Beyond the fence, a sign identifies the area as "Lynx Prairie—the E. Lucy Braun Preserve." Please keep on the trail and do not bring dogs; call the museum or the conservancy to arrange for visits by groups. Collect only by way of camera and memories.

Trail

A pileated woodpecker greeted me at the gate at 7:30 A.M. the last time I walked this trail. I saw it fly into the top of a pine overhead as I was crossing the cemetery. Every visit to this preserve has brought some special treat, and on that day, I got it before I even entered the gate.

Go beyond the fence opening and the National Park Service natural landmark plaque. The trail to the first opening cuts deeply into the Ohio black shale. Decades of naturalists' boots and runoff from the cemetery have created an outwash of shale at the entrance to the prairie. Aside from the myrtle, likely escaped from the grave-yard, and the poison ivy that you must step over, notice the kinds of trees alongside the trail—sassafras, Virginia pine, and chestnut oak, among others. These plants all thrive on the acidic soils that are derived from the carboniferous Ohio black shale.

Downslope, the trail opens up into the North Prairie, where the prairie grasses and forbs dominate. Look for Indian paintbrush in the spring and big bluestem and prairie dock in the summer. The sub-strate is Peebles dolomite, and the shallow soil does not hold mois-ture long.

Below the first opening, just before the trail crosses a small creek, some of the prairie or fen plants characteristic of wet calcar-eous soils can be seen: cowbane, spotted phlox, and golden ragwort, for example. This is also where the small, blue *Eupatorium* known as mist flower grows. Turn right at the first trail juncture to enter Elizabeth's Prairie. Look for rattlesnake master, green milkweed, American columbo, side-oats grama, tall coreopsis, and more.

Next is an opening called Dock Prairie because of the large amount of prairie dock there. Following extremely dry years, few may bloom, but they live for decades and bloom when conditions are right.

Pass through the pine woods beyond Dock Prairie, ignoring the short return trail to the left, and enter Occidentalis Prairie, named for its western sunflower. Look, too, for yellow flax. Beyond more pines is Petit Prairie, where shrubby St. John's-wort blooms next to the trail.

At the next trail junction, turn right to drop down to Latris Prairie. Here, in the late summer, the squatty scaly blazingstar thrives on the bare soil, and whorled rosinweed blooms in the calcareous soil in the moist bottom, often attracting many tiger swallowtail butterflies to its nectar.

Retrace your steps back uphill and go straight instead of entering the trail you came in on. Passing through a young woodland, you can sometimes hear water tumbling over a falls of yellow-stained, Silurian-age dolomite in the creek to the right.

On up the hill, tall blazingstar, a plant of wet prairies, grows almost in the trail. Where the trail reaches a "T", turn right to loop through Narrow Prairie, Warbler Prairie, Annette's Prairie, and Coneflower Prairie, in that order. Watch for whorled milkweed in Narrow Prairie in August, and in Warbler Prairie, look for blephilia in June. In the spring, shooting star grows along the trail just beyond Annette's Prairie where the trail drops to a small creek. Purple coneflower blooms in July and August in Coneflower Prairie, which is the opening beyond the exposed rock ledge.

Watch for clumps of Indiangrass with its yellow and brown inflorescence and for ox-eye with its yellow-orange sunflowerlike blossom. There will be something new to learn at each opening.

After making the loop to the four southern openings, turn right, passing the trail to the left that you came in on, and go north up and over a rise through the woods. Drop to a boardwalk that crosses a wetland and creek. One day when I passed this way, there was a box turtle with a badly infected eye in the creek bottom. Surrounding it, like elephants tending a sick pachyderm, were seven other box turtles.

Continue north, passing the two trails coming in from the left, and you will soon be back at North Prairie and the trail to the cemetery. You have just walked through a living museum with treasures to be protected and enjoyed.

Glossary of Terms

Cairn. A pile of stones erected as a memorial, a boundary marker, or a monument on the top of a mountain.

Calcareous. Composed of at least 50 percent calcium carbonate, such as limestone.

Calciphile. A plant that grows in and is adapted to an environment high in calcium carbonate.

Calcite. A common crystalline form of natural calcium carbonate. The basic constituent of limestone and many stalactites and stalagmites.

Dolomite. A magnesium-rich sedimentary rock resembling limestone.

Esker. A long, narrow ridge of gravel and sand desposited by a stream flowing in a tunnel in a decaying glacial ice sheet.

Fen. A grass-, sedge-, or reed-dominated peatland, often with some shrubs and small trees, developed under the influence of calcareous, mineral-rich, aerated water at or near the surface.

Forb. A term for any nongrassy herbaceous plant, used particularly for the broad-leaved plants of the prairies.

Glacial erratic. Boulders and stones of a different type of rock than the bedrock beneath, carried by and deposited on the land by a glacier. Often of igneous origin.

Gneiss. A foliated metamorphic rock similar in composition to granite.

Igneous rock. Rock formed by solidification from a molten or partially molten state.

Kame. A small, conical hill or short ridge of sand and gravel deposited during the melting of glacial ice.

Kettle lake. A lake in a depression in the land surface that was formed by the melting of glacial ice that had been entrapped in the ground moraine.

Mesophyte. A plant growing under medium or ordinary moisture conditions.

Moraine. An accumulation of boulders, stones, or other debris deposited by a glacier.

Ohio shale. A massive (10 to 2,000 feet thick), Devonian-age, noncalcareous, organic-rich shale which is black when freshly exposed but soon bleaches to tan or light gray at the surface.

Ordovician. Pertaining to the system of sedimentary rocks of the second period of the Paleozoic Era.

Peebles dolomite. A massive (50 to 100 feet thick), Silurian-age formation of fine-grained dolomite which remains gray or whitish on a weathered surface. Due to its open texture, weathering often produces a pronounced honeycomb effect.

Relic. A term applied to localized plants or plant communities which are thought to be survivors of an earlier geologic time.

Silurian. Pertaining to the system of sedimentary rocks of the third period of the Paleozoic Era.

Stalactite. A cylindrical or conical deposit, usually of calcite or aragonite, projecting downward from the roof of a cavern as a result of dripping mineral-rich water.

Sugar bush. A grove of sugar maples used as a source of sap for the making of maple syrup or maple sugar.

Xeric. Characterized by or adapted to an extremely dry habitat.

Books from The Countryman Press and Backcountry Publications

The Countryman Press and Backcountry Publications, long known for fine books on travel and outdoor recreation, offer a range of practical and readable manuals.

Walks & Rambles Series:

Walks & Rambles on Cape Cod and the Islands, $11.00
Walks & Rambles in Dutchess and Putnam Counties, $11.00
Walks & Rambles in Westchester & Fairfield Counties, 2nd Ed., $11.00
Walks & Rambles in Rhode Island, 2nd Ed., $11.00
More Walks & Rambles in Rhode Island, $11.00
Walks & Rambles on the Delmarva Peninsula, $11.00
Walks & Rambles in the Upper Connecticut River Valley, $10.00

Other Books on Walking:

Bird Walks in Rhode Island, $9.95
Walk to Your Heart's Content, by Norman Ford, $14.95

Hiking Series:

Fifty Hikes in the Adirondacks, $13.00
Fifty Hikes in Central New York, $12.00
Fifty Hikes in Central Pennsylvania, $12.00
Fifty Hikes in Connecticut, $12.00
Fifty Hikes in Eastern Pennsylvania, $12.00
Fifty Hikes in the Hudson Valley, $14.00
Fifty Hikes in Lower Michigan, $13.00
Fifty Hikes in Massachusetts, $13.00
Fifty Hikes in New Jersey, $13.00
Fifty Hikes in Northern Maine, $12.00
Fifty Hikes in Northern Virginia, $13.00
Fifty Hikes in Ohio, $13.00
Fifty Hikes in Southern Maine, $12.00
Fifty Hikes in Vermont, $12.00
Fifty Hikes in Western New York, $13.00
Fifty Hikes in Western Pennsylvania, $12.00
Fifty Hikes in the White Mountains, $13.00
Fifty More Hikes in New Hampshire, $13.00

We offer many more books on hiking, walking, fishing, and canoeing plus books on travel, nature, and many other subjects. Our titles are available in bookshops and in many sporting goods stores, or they may be ordered directly from the publisher. Shipping and handling costs are $2.50 for 1 book, 50¢ for each additional book. To order, or for a complete catalog, please write to The Countryman Press, Inc., P.O. Box 175, Dept. APC, Woodstock, VT 05091, or call our toll-free number, (800) 245-4151. Prices and availability are subject to change.